The Book On

The Cookbook for Cannibals

Feast of the Forgotten: A Culinary Guide to the Taboo

The Book On Series

Eleanor V. Braun

Published by The Book On Publishing, 2025.

First edition. October 27, 2025

Website: https://thebookon.ca

Substack: https://thebookonpublishing.substack.com/

The Book On The Cookbook for Cannibals: Feast of the Forgotten: A Culinary Guide to the Taboo

First edition. October 27, 2025

ISBN: 978-1-997795-08-7

Written by Eleanor V. Braun

Other Books in The Book On Series

Table of Contents

Dedication

For those whose own appetites have consumed — and those still pretending they haven't tasted the same thing.

Chapter 1: Origins of Anthropophagy: A Historical Overview

The first lie they teach you about cannibalism is that it's aberrant. The second lie follows quickly: that it belongs to "them"—the distant, the primitive, the morally bankrupt others who exist outside civilization's warm light. Both lies serve the same function. They let us sleep at night, convinced that the consumption of human flesh represents a deviation from human nature rather than a manifestation of it. But the archaeological record doesn't care about our comfort. Neither does history. When you examine the evidence without flinching, what emerges isn't a story of occasional madness but a practice so widespread across geography and time that calling it aberrant becomes the real distortion.

The oldest confirmed evidence of anthropophagy dates back roughly 800,000 years to Gran Dolina cave in Spain's Atapuerca Mountains. These weren't modern humans. Homo antecessor processed the bones of their own kind with the same systematic efficiency they applied to deer and rabbits—scraping, breaking, and extracting marrow. The cut marks tell an unambiguous story. They ate each other, not in frenzied desperation, but as routine protein acquisition. This predates Homo sapiens by half a million years, which means that before we became human in any sense we'd recognize, our ancestors had already normalized consuming their own species. The practice is older than language, older than symbolic thought, older than everything we use to define humanity. You can't dismiss this as cultural pathology when it exists before culture itself.

The Neanderthal Question and What It Reveals

The Neanderthal sites compound the problem for anyone seeking easy moral categories. Moula-Guercy cave in France, El Sidrón cave in Spain, Krapina in Croatia—the pattern repeats. Neanderthal remains showing identical processing to animal prey: defleshing, bone marrow extraction, and even evidence of cooking. At El Sidrón, genetic analysis revealed that a family group consumed their own relatives. Twelve individuals, connected by blood, were systematically butchered. The bones were fractured to access marrow, the tongues removed, the brains extracted through the foramen magnum—the opening at the skull's base. This wasn't symbolic. This was efficiency. They knew exactly how to maximize nutritional yield from a human body because they'd done it before.

What troubles us isn't just that this happened. It's the implication of technical competence. These weren't desperate survivors clawing at corpses. The sophistication of processing suggests transmitted knowledge, practiced technique, and cultural continuity. Someone taught someone else how to do this properly. Which means communities existed where the butchering of humans qualified as necessary knowledge, passed down like fire-making or tool-shaping. The Neanderthals lived in small bands, perhaps twenty to thirty individuals. In a group that size, eating your own wasn't an abstraction. You knew their voice, their habits, and whether they laughed easily. Then you processed their remains with professional competence. This is what scalds: the coexistence of intimacy and consumption, the absence of apparent cognitive dissonance.

By the time anatomically modern humans spread across the globe, cannibalism had already established itself as part of our inherited behavioral repertoire. The practice appears on every inhabited continent. Papua New Guinea's Fore people consumed deceased relatives until the practice was banned in the 1960s, with prion disease providing the brutal verification that yes, they'd been eating human brain tissue for generations. In Fiji, cannibalism continued into the late 19th century with sufficient regularity that they developed culinary terminology—"bokola" for human flesh specifically. The Anasazi of the American Southwest left archaeological sites at Cowboy Wash showing classic signs of anthropophagy from around 1150 CE: pot-polished bones, thermal alteration, and identical processing to faunal remains. The Aztecs would later institutionalize the practice on an industrial scale. The geographic distribution alone demolishes any theory of isolated aberration.

Motivational Categories and Their Insufficient Boundaries

Anthropologists, desperate to impose order on this ubiquity, created taxonomies. Survival cannibalism: the Donner Party, the Uruguayan Air Force Flight 571, the siege of Leningrad. Ritual cannibalism: consuming enemies to absorb their strength, eating kin to honor the dead. Gustatory cannibalism: the category we refuse to examine closely because it suggests preference rather than compulsion. Pathological cannibalism: the domain of individual psychosis, where we safely contain Jeffrey Dahmer and Issei Sagawa. These categories provide psychological comfort through the illusion of comprehension. But they leak at the boundaries. They can't account for the Gran Dolina efficiency or the Neanderthal technical competence that predates any ritual framework we can imagine.

The Fore people claimed their mortuary cannibalism honored the dead, preventing the body's decay and incorporating the deceased into the living community. This fits neatly into "ritual" until you examine the distribution pattern: they preferentially consumed female relatives and children, while adult males received traditional burial. Then it looks less like universal honor and more like strategic nutrition hidden behind ritual justification. The Aztec priests claimed religious necessity, feeding captives' hearts to Huitzilopochtli to sustain the sun's journey. Then the Spanish chroniclers noted how the limbs of sacrificed captives disappeared into the city's cooking pots, distributed to noble families who'd provided the sacrifice. The theological justification coexisted with nutritional practicality. Which was the primary motivation? The question itself may be wrong. Perhaps they're not separate categories but simultaneous truths, and our need to separate them reveals our discomfort more than their reality.

What the categories obscure is the functionality's banality. A human body contains approximately 81,500 calories—roughly forty days of survival for one person at minimal activity levels. The skeletal muscle mass of a 180-pound individual yields about 50 pounds of consumable protein. In nutritional terms, humans qualify as large game. Not optimal—higher risk than deer, more complex emotional processing required—but viable. The Paleolithic groups working in the Atapuerca caves weren't philosophizing about the sacred and profane. They solved a protein problem with available resources. The same calculation is repeated across hemispheres and millennia because the math doesn't change. We are, objectively, edible.

The Colonial Gaze and Manufactured Monstrosity

Here's where the historical narrative gets deliberately corrupted. European colonizers needed cannibalism to justify subjugation.

Columbus's logbook references "canibales"—a term derived from "Carib"—almost immediately upon landing. He had no direct evidence. He relied on enemy tribes' accusations, which conveniently transformed potential trading partners into subhuman monsters requiring civilizing violence. The pattern repeated wherever Europeans encountered resistance: Africa, the Pacific Islands, and the Americas. Describe the indigenous population as cannibalistic, and suddenly, invasion becomes salvation, slavery becomes rescue, genocide becomes an unfortunate necessity.

The Reverend John Williams died in Erromango in 1839, killed by islanders tired of missionary pressure. His death immediately spawned lurid accounts of cannibalism, with elaborate details about cooking methods and consumption. The accounts varied wildly, contradicted each other, and included anatomical impossibilities. Didn't matter. The story served its function: reinforcing European moral superiority and indigenous savagery. Later evidence suggested the islanders simply killed Williams for being an aggressive annoyance, no consumption involved. But the cannibal narrative had already achieved escape velocity, shaping policy and public opinion for decades.

This manufactured horror served such effective propaganda purposes that it obscured actual anthropophagy where it existed. When anthropologist William Arens published "The Man-Eating Myth" in 1979, arguing that reliable evidence for cannibalism was surprisingly scarce, he wasn't entirely wrong about the colonial distortions. He was just mistaken about the underlying reality. The archaeological evidence, the genetic markers of prion disease in the Fore, the contemporary accounts by indigenous people themselves describing their own practices—these accumulated too heavily to dismiss. What Arens correctly identified was the weaponization of cannibalism as a colonial justification. What he missed was that beneath the propaganda, the practice existed with sufficient frequency to warrant serious examination rather than wholesale skepticism.

The colonial distortion damaged anthropology's ability to examine anthropophagy honestly for generations. Researchers feared accusations of racism if they documented it, or of gullibility if they relied on potentially contaminated sources. This created a silence more insidious than the propaganda. When you can't discuss a practice clearly, you can't understand its actual patterns, functions, or meanings. The silence protected neither indigenous peoples nor historical truth. It just ensured that pop culture filled the vacuum with Hannibal Lecter and Texas Chainsaw Massacre—projecting Western pathology while claiming to depict universal human darkness.

Facing What the Evidence Demands

The archaeological and historical record requires us to acknowledge an uncomfortable proposition: anthropophagy isn't abnormal human behavior. It's an optional human behavior that becomes activated under specific ecological, social, and cultural conditions. Those conditions have occurred repeatedly across human history with sufficient frequency that every major geographic population has likely engaged in the practice at some point. This doesn't mean humans are "naturally" cannibalistic in the sense of preferring human flesh. It means we're naturally omnivorous with sufficient behavioral flexibility to incorporate conspecific consumption when circumstances render it advantageous or necessary.

What separates modern industrial societies from our ancestors isn't moral evolution. It's surplus. We have sufficient alternative protein that we can afford the luxury of categorical prohibition. The taboo against cannibalism feels visceral, innate, universal. It's not. It's cultural programming running on top of behavioral flexibility, and it's newer than we pretend. Medieval Europe's medicinal cannibalism—corpse medicine, mummy powder, human skull preparations—continued into the 18th century among the educated elite who publicly condemned indigenous peoples for identical practices. The taboo's intensity reflects how recently we needed it, how thin the cultural membrane separating acceptable from unacceptable actually is.

This first chapter establishes the foundation for everything that follows: anthropophagy isn't an exception requiring special explanation. It's a default option in the human behavioral toolkit, activated across history with predictable regularity. Understanding its origins means accepting that the practice precedes and transcends the moral frameworks we've constructed to contain it. The archaeological evidence from Gran Dolina to Moula-Guercy to Cowboy Wash doesn't document aberration. It documents our species being exactly what it is—behaviorally flexible, nutritionally pragmatic, and capable of normalizing almost any practice when survival or culture demands it. The real question isn't why cannibalism happened. It's why we're so desperate to pretend it didn't.

The Starvation Threshold and Its Predictable Appearance

Here's what every famine teaches us: the taboo has a caloric threshold. Cross it, and the prohibition dissolves with surprising speed. The siege of Leningrad lasted 872 days. Soviet documents, declassified decades later, record over 2,000 arrests for cannibalism during the blockade. The actual number was certainly higher—those are just the cases that resulted in detention. NKVD reports describe a market economy: flesh sold by type, pricing structures, and quality gradations. This wasn't chaos. It was a systematized response to systematic starvation. The Chinese famines of 1958-1962 produced similar patterns across provinces. Official silence, survivor testimony, and the sudden appearance of euphemistic phrases in local dialect that everyone understood. When people ate tree bark, then leather, then each other, they followed a progression so predictable you could plot it on a graph.

The Holodomor in Ukraine, the Bengal famine, the siege of Ma'arra during the First Crusade, where Frankish chroniclers documented their own side's consumption of enemy dead—the pattern repeats because the biological pressure is identical. Humans can survive roughly three weeks without food before organ failure begins. The body starts consuming itself: muscle tissue, then organs. By week two, cognitive function deteriorates enough that moral frameworks start fragmenting. The taboo against cannibalism feels absolute until you're watching someone die of starvation while a corpse lies available. Then the taboo reveals itself as a luxury good, affordable only when alternatives exist.

What disturbs isn't that starving people ate the dead. It's how quickly communities developed protocols for it. Who could be eaten, who couldn't. Whether killing for meat became acceptable or only the consumption of those already dead. The fact that these discussions happened—that rules emerged—demonstrates something we'd rather not see: humans can normalize anything given sufficient pressure and time. Not just individuals cracking under extreme duress, but communities arriving at collective decisions, establishing boundaries, creating the social infrastructure around a practice that theoretically represented civilization's absolute limit.

The Donner Party is taught as a cautionary tale about poor planning and winter timing. Less discussed: they didn't descend into random cannibalism. They created rules. No family members. The dead only, not the dying. This wasn't madness. It was ethics under pressure, morality adapted to circumstances that rendered previous moral frameworks obsolete. What does it mean that humans trapped by snowfall could construct a new ethical system in weeks, complete with boundaries and enforcement? It means the moral architecture isn't load-bearing. It's decorative. Strip away the surplus that makes it affordable, and humans rebuild ethics from available materials. Sometimes those materials include the recently deceased.

The Medicinal Cannibalism Nobody Wants to Claim

Europe's corpse medicine lasted longer than the indigenous practices it condemned. Egyptian mummy, ground to powder and consumed as a cure-all. "Mellified man"—corpses preserved in honey, aged for decades, then sold as medicine. Human skull preparations for epilepsy. Blood drinking for vigor. Fat rendered from executed criminals was applied to wounds. This wasn't fringe practice. It was standard pharmacology, appearing in official dispensatories into the 1700s. The Royal Society—that beacon of Enlightenment rationality—included members who consumed and recommended human skull preparations. King Charles II of England kept a private stock of "King's Drops," made from human skulls, which he took regularly.

The cognitive dissonance is instructive. The same culture horrified by New World cannibalism maintained an extensive commercial infrastructure for human body products. Executioners in Germany held a legal monopoly on corpse harvesting, selling remains to apothecaries as a lucrative side business. The market was sophisticated enough to discriminate by cause of death—violent death supposedly imbued flesh with particular properties—and by body part. The skull of someone who died peacefully held a different medicinal value than the skull of someone executed. They developed an entire epistemology around consuming human remains while maintaining that consuming human remains was precisely what separated civilization from savagery.

The distinction they drew was transparent: medicinal consumption had a theoretical framework, textual justification, and Latin terminology. It was "Mumia vera Aegyptica" in the dispensatory, not "eating dead people" in plain language. The linguistic elevation did the work of moral separation. Call it medicine, wrap it in Galenic theory, charge accordingly, and suddenly you're not engaged in anthropophagy at all. You're practicing pharmaceutical science. This is how humans operate: we can engage in any practice as long as we construct sufficient conceptual distance from what we're actually doing. The Europeans weren't cannibals because they had doctors' orders and price lists. The Caribs were cannibals because they were honest about it.

Warfare, Tactical Terror, and the Instrumental Body

Then there's anthropophagy as psychological warfare—the body weaponized through its consumption. The Māori traditionally consumed defeated enemies not primarily for nutrition but for "mana"—spiritual power and prestige. But they also understood the tactical value of reputation. If your enemies believe you'll eat them, they fight differently. Terror has battlefield utility. The Aztec practice served multiple functions simultaneously: religious obligation, political theater, nutritional distribution, and tactical intimidation. The Spanish conquistadors were genuinely horrified, but also genuinely terrified. The Aztecs knew this. They'd built an empire partly on that knowledge.

Modern militaries understand this calculation even if they don't employ the practice. Psychological operations aim to break the enemy's will before physical engagement. Cannibalism represents the ultimate psychological operation—consumption as complete erasure, denial of even burial rites, transformation of enemy into literal shit. It's brutality with semiotic efficiency. You don't need to eat many enemies to gain reputational benefit. A few well-publicized instances create strategic value far exceeding the caloric yield.

The Japanese soldiers in World War II who consumed Allied POWs weren't operating under starvation conditions in every case. In some instances, alternative food existed. What they gained wasn't primarily nutritional. It was the assertion of absolute dominance, the demonstration that enemy bodies held less value than animal carcasses, the psychological fracturing that comes from being reduced to meat. When you've eaten someone, you've achieved a level of dominion that mere killing doesn't confer. You've incorporated them. They've become a substrate for your continued existence. It's degradation that extends beyond death into biological transformation.

This instrumental anthropophagy—using consumption as a tool rather than feeding as a goal—reveals something darker than starvation cannibalism. Starvation cannibalism at least makes biological sense. We understand the equation. But tactical cannibalism requires calculating that the psychological damage inflicted through consumption outweighs the risks and costs of the practice itself. It requires believing that eating your enemy produces a strategic advantage. And throughout history, groups have made exactly that calculation, which means they were probably right. The practice wouldn't have persisted across cultures if it lacked efficacy.

The Prion Time Bomb and Evolution's Long Memory

The biological evidence suggests we've been doing this long enough that natural selection has noticed. Kuru disease devastated the Fore people of Papua New Guinea—progressive neurological degeneration caused by prions in consumed brain tissue. But research revealed something else: some Fore individuals carried genetic mutations that provided resistance to prion diseases. These mutations don't arise randomly. They emerge through selection pressure, which requires repeated exposure over generations. The Fore had been practicing mortuary cannibalism long enough that their gene pool developed partial adaptation to the primary risk.

This wasn't unique to the Fore. Similar prion-resistant genetic variants appear in other populations at frequencies suggesting historical selection pressure. Not universal—the protection isn't complete, and the practice wasn't constant enough everywhere to drive fixation. But present at rates that make sense only if anthropophagy occurred with sufficient regularity that prion disease became relevant evolutionary pressure. Our DNA carries the receipts. We've been eating each other long enough that some populations have evolved partial immunity to the primary pathogen that the practice transmits.

The kuru epidemic itself demonstrates how cultural practice can override biological warning signs. The Fore knew something was wrong—they called it the "laughing sickness" because of the pathological giggling it caused. The disease was obviously fatal, obviously connected to their mortuary practices even before outside researchers identified the mechanism. They continued anyway. Cultural obligation outweighed biological risk, even obvious and fatal risk, for decades. This is the thing about human behavior: we're not actually very rational. We don't automatically cease practices that harm us if those practices carry sufficient social meaning. We rationalize, compartmentalize, and minimize. We do what culture demands, even when empirical evidence says stop.

What the Silence Protects

Academic anthropology spent decades navigating between two errors: the colonial exaggeration that saw cannibalism everywhere as justification for subjugation, and the postcolonial overcorrection that denied its existence to protect indigenous peoples from racist stereotyping. Both positions sacrificed accuracy for political utility. The truth—that anthropophagy occurred with moderate frequency across diverse cultures, motivated by various combinations of necessity, ritual, and preference—got lost between propaganda extremes.

This silence protected no one. It certainly didn't protect the Fore people, whose mortuary practices went unexamined until prion disease created a public health emergency. It didn't preserve historical understanding because you can't comprehend a culture while deliberately ignoring its actual practices. It didn't even protect indigenous peoples from racism, because the absence of scholarly discussion just meant pop culture filled the vacuum with lurid fiction bearing no relationship to ethnographic reality. The silence was cowardice disguised as sensitivity, and it degraded anthropology's ability to examine human behavioral diversity honestly.

We need to be able to say: yes, some cultures practiced anthropophagy, for reasons ranging from nutrition to ritual to tactical intimidation. And: this doesn't make them morally inferior or less human. And: understanding the practice's frequency and motivations tells us important things about human behavioral flexibility and cultural variability. These aren't contradictory positions. They're all simultaneously true. But we've constructed a discourse where acknowledging the first point feels like conceding the second, so we avoid discussing any of it clearly.

The cost of that avoidance is ignorance about our own nature. We are the species that can normalize almost anything, given the right combination of necessity, time, and cultural scaffolding. Anthropophagy isn't the exception that proves we can transcend our nature. It's the example that proves we don't have a fixed nature to transcend. We have behavioral possibility space, and cannibalism lives comfortably within it, available for activation whenever circumstances align. That's not a moral judgment. It's a biological fact. And understanding it requires looking directly at evidence we'd rather not see, then accepting what that evidence actually demonstrates about the animals we are.

Chapter 2: Rituals of the Flesh: Cannibalism in Ancient Cultures

The temple priests of Tenochtitlan maintained detailed records. Not of battles or harvest yields, but of procurement schedules. How many captives from which tributary states? Which festivals required what quantities? The logistics of keeping fifty to eighty thousand bodies moving through ceremonial disassembly each year demanded administrative competence that would impress modern supply chain managers. This wasn't savagery. This was bureaucracy applied to human consumption with such systematic efficiency that it created economic infrastructure. The Aztec empire didn't just permit ritual cannibalism—it built its political architecture around it. Subject cities paid their tribute in human bodies. The empire's expansion wasn't primarily territorial; it was agricultural in the most disturbing sense. They were farming people.

What distinguishes ritual cannibalism from its other manifestations isn't the presence of ceremony—that's the surface reading, the tourist understanding. The distinction lies in integration. Ritual anthropophagy becomes structural. It weaves itself into cosmology, governance, and social hierarchy so thoroughly that removing it would collapse the entire system. The Aztecs believed the sun required human blood to rise each morning. Not metaphorically. Not as poetry. As a mechanical necessity, the way an engine involves oil. Their priests weren't conducting religious theater; they were performing what they understood as maintenance on reality itself. Miss too many sacrifices and the universe stops functioning. When cannibalism reaches this level of institutionalization, it transcends individual acts and becomes a civilizational operating system. The question isn't whether specific people chose to participate—the question becomes whether you could even conceive of a society that didn't.

The Architecture of Sacred Consumption

The Wari' people of Brazil's western Amazon practiced endocannibalism until contact with missionaries in the 1960s forced cessation. But here's what the sanitized anthropological accounts miss: they didn't just eat their dead relatives. They ate them while weeping. They described the act as profoundly painful, viscerally revolting, yet absolutely mandatory. The ritual required that close kin consume the roasted flesh while actively grieving, often vomiting from emotional distress, even as they continued eating. This wasn't honor or reverence in any sense we'd recognize. It was an obligation performed at the intersection of love and horror. The Wari themselves reported finding the practice disgusting. They did it anyway because their cosmology demanded it—the dead couldn't transition properly otherwise. Western observers wanted to see dignity and respect; the Wari' experienced traumatic duty.

This reveals something critical about ritual cannibalism that the academic literature consistently fumbles: the participants often experience profound ambivalence. We expect either enthusiastic embrace or horror-struck refusal, but most ritual anthropophagy occupies neither pole. Instead, it exists in a space of complicated necessity where cultural mandate overrides individual revulsion. The Fore women of Papua New Guinea, who consumed deceased relatives' brains during mortuary feasts, developed kuru—a fatal prion disease. They knew something was wrong. The connection between funerary practices and the shaking sickness became increasingly obvious as epidemiologists documented it in the 1950s. Yet the practice continued for years afterward because abandoning it meant abandoning their understanding of proper death, proper kinship, proper humanity. Some cultural structures demand such profound investment that even fatal consequences don't immediately break the system.

The Tupinambá of coastal Brazil created something even more complex: ceremonial consumption of enemies that required months of preparation and the full cooperation of the victim. When warriors captured enemies in battle, they didn't kill them immediately. Instead, they brought captives home, gave them wives, and integrated them into village life for months or sometimes years. The captive lived as a community member, fully aware of their eventual fate. Then, on the designated day, the entire village assembled. The captive, painted and decorated, participated in their own ritual execution—sometimes even requesting it be done properly according to form. Only after ceremonial club death did the consumption begin, distributed according to complex social rules about who could eat which portions. The system required that everyone—captors, captives, and the community—perform assigned roles in a choreographed sequence.

This wasn't savagery. This was civilization expressing itself through anthropophagous ritual so elaborate it makes contemporary criminal justice systems look improvisational.

Sacred Economies and Flesh Distribution

When the Spanish conquistadors documented Aztec practices, they focused on temple spectacle—the drama of hearts torn from living chests, blood cascading down pyramid steps. They missed the economic substrate. After ceremonial sacrifice, bodies didn't vanish into priestly mysteries. They entered distribution networks. Limbs went to noble houses, often to warriors who'd captured the victim. Torsos fed temple functionaries. Internal organs had designated recipients according to rank and role. The system operated like any other administrative mechanism for resource allocation, except that the resource happened to be human meat. Bernal Díaz del Castillo, who marched with Cortés, documented markets where human flesh sold alongside other protein sources, priced according to cut and quality. The economic integration was so complete that when the Spanish banned the practice, they created genuine supply shocks in protein-dependent markets.

This wasn't unique to Mesoamerica. The Fijian tribal confederations of the pre-colonial period maintained parallel systems, though decentralized. Chiefs received specific portions as tribute, marking status through consumption rights. A chief's prestige correlated directly with how much bokola—their specific term for human flesh— he could command. When rival chiefs made peace, the treaty often included flesh-sharing to cement a political alliance. The ritual consumption created obligation networks as binding as marriage ties or trade agreements. Some anthropologists argue these weren't true "economies" because spiritual significance supposedly negated material calculation. But the participants kept a detailed accounting. They knew exactly who owed what to whom, which portions conveyed which status markers, and how consumption rights transferred through inheritance. Call it sacred if you want; it still functioned as a market.

The Korowai people of southeastern Papua practiced both endo- and exocannibalism into the 21st century, despite Indonesian government prohibition. Their system reveals how sacred and strategic collapse

21

into each other until the categories become meaningless. They consumed khakhua—male witches who supposedly ate people from the inside through magical means. When someone died from a disease, the community identified which male had cursed them, killed him, and consumed his body in retribution. This looks like pure cosmology until you notice the pattern: accused witches were almost always men without strong kinship networks, often those from neighboring territories without local political protection. The supernatural explanation provided legitimacy, but the practice functioned as population management and territorial consolidation. Sacred purpose and strategic advantage weren't separate motivations—they were the same thing expressed in different vocabularies.

Theological Necessity and Cosmological Mandate

The Aztec cosmos didn't just permit human sacrifice—it required it under threat of universal annihilation. Their creation myth held that the gods themselves had sacrificed their own blood to create the sun and humanity. This established an eternal debt. Humans existed only because divine blood had paid the price, and the only possible repayment was reciprocal sacrifice. The debt couldn't be forgiven because it was ontological, not moral. You can't negotiate with the conditions of existence itself. What made this particularly binding was the historical narrative: previous suns had failed when humans didn't fulfill their obligations, plunging the world into destruction. The current sun, the Fifth Sun, remained provisional. It would continue only as long as the blood debt was serviced. This wasn't religious paranoia; it was theology functioning as physics. Miss payments and reality collapses.

The genius of this system—and yes, it was genius in its coherence—was that it made imperial expansion a cosmic imperative. The Aztec empire needed constant warfare, not primarily for territory but for captives. More captives meant more sacrifices, which meant more cosmic security. Conquered peoples had to provide victims for their own existential continuation. The empire told subject states: We're not oppressing you, we're saving reality, and you're contributing to the salvation that benefits everyone, including yourselves. It's almost impossible to rebel against a system that frames its violence as metaphysical maintenance. The closest modern parallel might be nuclear deterrence logic, where strategic planners describe potential mass death as "credible commitment to stability." Both systems transform horror into necessity through totalizing frameworks that admit no outside perspective.

The Maori of pre-colonial New Zealand operated under different cosmological rules but similar necessities. They believed mana— spiritual power—concentrated in the human head. Consuming an enemy's brain didn't just demonstrate victory; it transferred their mana to the consumer and, through him, to his tribe. Chiefs who'd consumed many enemies became repositories of accumulated power, both spiritual and political. This created an arms race of consumption where not eating defeated enemies meant leaving power on the battlefield for someone else to claim. The practice wasn't optional for ambitious leaders. You either absorbed enemy mana through ritual consumption or accepted permanent subordinate status. The cosmology created strategic compulsion: consume or be consumed, not just literally but politically.

The Ritual's Burden on Participants

What the anthropological accounts consistently sanitize is the psychological cost. The Wari' elders, interviewed decades after abandoning endocannibalism, still wept describing it. Not from nostalgia. From trauma. They explained that forcing yourself to consume someone you loved while your grief was fresh created wounds that never fully healed. The ritual demanded this timing specifically—you had to eat them while you still mourned intensely, while their absence felt visceral. Waiting until grief faded would be disrespectful, as it would suggest you hadn't loved them enough. So you consumed their flesh while sobbing, often becoming physically ill, always psychologically scarred. The community acknowledged this cost but insisted it was necessary. The dead required it. The living provided it. But no one pretended it was easy or natural or anything other than a traumatic obligation.

The Aghoris of India, who practice cannibalism at cremation grounds even today, describe similar burdens through a different framework. They consume partially cremated human flesh as meditation on impermanence and the illusory nature of disgust. The practice is meant to shatter conventional boundaries between pure and impure,

23

sacred and profane. But interviews with practitioners reveal that it doesn't stop being horrifying. The revulsion doesn't evaporate through a philosophical framework. Instead, they experience revulsion and continue anyway, using the discomfort as proof that they've transcended ordinary limitations. The practice works precisely because it remains difficult. If it became easy, it would lose spiritual utility. This means every instance requires fresh courage, fresh violation of deep instinct, fresh psychological cost. The ritual doesn't adapt to them; they must continuously adapt to it.

The complexity multiplies when ritual cannibalism creates permanent social roles. Aztec priests who performed sacrifices and managed flesh distribution couldn't simply retire. Once initiated into that priesthood, you carried knowledge and responsibility that isolated you from ordinary social relationships. You'd eaten hundreds of people. You'd memorized the proper ceremonies. You understood the cosmic machinery in ways that made normal concerns seem trivial. Former practitioners from various cultures describe similar permanent alterations—not regret exactly, but fundamental change. You can't unknow how human flesh tastes, can't un-experience the weight of hearts in your hands, can't forget the specific sounds and smells. The ritual creates permanent witnesses who must carry their experiences in contexts that may no longer have language for them. When the Spanish banned Aztec practices, they didn't just end a religious system; they created thousands of people who'd built their identities around actions their new world considered monstrous.

The archaeological and historical record makes this unavoidable: ritual cannibalism wasn't a deviation from civilization but one of its expressions. It emerged independently across continents, integrated into complex social systems, survived for centuries, and shaped human culture in ways still echoing. The practices revealed remarkable organizational sophistication, theological coherence, and social complexity. They also inflicted profound individual cost, created traumatic obligations, and required participants to violate their own instincts in the service of a cultural mandate. Both things are true simultaneously. The horror and the sophistication don't cancel each other out—they coexist, which is precisely what makes ritual anthropophagy so disturbing to examine honestly. Monsters didn't commit it. It was committed by people building civilizations according to their best understanding of cosmic necessity. That might actually be worse.

The Collapse Point: When Systems End

Here's what nobody wants to discuss: most ritual cannibalism didn't end because participants experienced moral awakening. It ended because an external force made continuation impossible. The Wari didn't spontaneously decide their mortuary practices violated human dignity—Brazilian missionaries and government officials made continuation illegal and socially untenable. The Fore didn't abandon their funerary feasts through ethical evolution—the kuru epidemic simply made the mortality rate unsustainable, and even then, some communities needed years to fully stop. The Aztec system didn't collapse from internal reform—Spanish conquest and forced conversion dismantled it at sword-point. When anthropologists describe these endings as "cultural evolution" or "modernization," they're papering over violence with progress narratives. These systems ended through defeat, not enlightenment.

This matters because it complicates our comfortable stories about moral development. We want to believe that humans naturally trend toward less violent, more "civilized" practices—that we collectively recognize barbarism and abandon it. But the evidence suggests otherwise. Ritual cannibalism persisted not because people were ignorant but because the systems worked. They provided coherent explanations for death, suffering, and cosmic order. They created social bonds and political structures. They made sense of the senseless. The Aztec empire didn't eat people because they failed to understand ethics; they did it because their ethical system, their entire framework for understanding right action, demanded it. When that system ended, it wasn't transcended—it was destroyed and replaced with a different system that we happen to find less disturbing. But ask yourself honestly: in four hundred years, what practices we consider normal now will seem equally monstrous? The moral certainty we feel about their barbarism should terrify us about our own.

The transition periods reveal the most. When the Fijian confederations began abandoning bokola in the mid-1800s under missionary pressure, it didn't happen cleanly. Some chiefs converted to Christianity but privately maintained consumption rights, hiding the practice while publicly performing conversion. Others split the difference—they'd consume enemies killed in warfare but not those who died naturally, as if the source of death somehow altered the moral calculus. Younger generations, educated in mission schools, often felt genuine revulsion toward practices their parents considered a sacred obligation. This created intergenerational trauma as profound as the practice itself. Parents who'd built identity around warrior prowess and ritual consumption faced children who saw them as savages. The children, meanwhile, lost connection to cosmologies that had provided meaning for millennia, often without gaining full access to the Christian frameworks meant to replace them. They became people between worlds, fluent in neither.

The Korowai case is even more instructive because it extends into living memory. When Indonesian authorities and Western missionaries pushed into their territory in the 1970s and 80s, they didn't just ban khakhua consumption—they invalidated the entire cosmological framework. If you can't kill witches who eat people from the inside, how do you explain why people die from mysterious illnesses? The Korowai had a coherent system: disease meant witchcraft, witchcraft meant identifying the witch, identification meant execution and consumption, consumption meant justice and deterrence. Remove that chain and you're left with unexplained death, unresolved grief, and no mechanism for restoration. The authorities offered modern medicine and Christian theology as a replacement. Still, these required decades to integrate and didn't address the immediate emotional and social needs that the old system had served. Some Korowai adapted by identifying witches but turning them over to the police instead of executing them, attempting to preserve the diagnostic framework while outsourcing the punishment. Others simply continued the practice covertly, reasoning that external authorities who didn't understand their cosmos had no legitimate jurisdiction over it.

The Mirror They Hold Up

The academic tendency is to study ritual cannibalism as a historical curiosity, something extinct peoples did in less enlightened times. This is cowardice. These practices force us to confront uncomfortable truths about how cultural systems shape moral reasoning. The Aztec priests who efficiently processed thousands of bodies annually weren't psychopaths—they were conscientious professionals fulfilling sacred duties. The Wari' parents who forced themselves to eat their children's flesh while grieving weren't monsters—they were loving relatives performing what their culture defined as a final obligation. The Fijian chiefs who calculated prestige through consumption quotas weren't simple brutes—they were political operators navigating complex status hierarchies. Every one of them operated within systems that made their actions not just permissible but mandatory, even virtuous.

We are not different in kind. We simply have different systems. The logistical precision that impresses us in Aztec sacrifice administration—the same precision operates in our industrial agriculture, our healthcare bureaucracies, our military operations. The cultural mandate that made Wari' endocannibalism mandatory despite individual revulsion operates in our own obligations and taboos, just attached to different acts. The cosmological frameworks that made consuming enemies metaphysically necessary for the Maori have parallels in every ideology that justifies violence through appeals to larger necessity. The structure is identical; only the content differs. This doesn't excuse anything, but it should humble us. The distance between their practices and our certainties is narrower than we pretend.

Consider how we discuss factory farming, where billions of animals with measurable capacity for suffering live in conditions we'd consider torture if applied to humans. The system operates with Aztec-level logistical sophistication, creates economic dependencies throughout society, and persists despite widespread knowledge of its cruelties because—like ritual cannibalism—it's become structurally integrated. We have cosmological justifications too, though we call them different things: nutritional necessity, economic efficiency, cultural tradition, natural order. When future generations judge us, will they see moral actors making difficult choices in complex systems? Or will they see people who knew better but continued anyway because the entire structure of their civilization was built around practices they didn't want to examine? The Aztec priests probably wondered the same thing.

The point isn't moral relativism—some practices genuinely are more harmful than others, cause more suffering, deserve condemnation. But the fact is also not smug superiority. Ritual cannibalism in its various forms reveals how thoroughly culture can override individual conscience, how completely cosmology can justify horror, how deeply systems can integrate practices that destroy the people performing them. Every civilization manages this trick with something. The cannibalistic ones are just more obvious about it, more viscerally disturbing in ways that prevent easy dismissal. They make us look directly at the gap between what humans will do and what humans, in other contexts, know is wrong. That gap exists everywhere. Ritual anthropophagy just has the decency to make it visible.

Chapter 3: Survival Tactics: Cannibalism in Extreme Conditions

The lifeboat leaked. Not catastrophically, but enough that the eighteen men aboard spent every conscious moment bailing with anything that held water—boots, hats, cupped hands. They'd been adrift for nineteen days when Thomas Dudley, captain of the yacht *Mignonette*, proposed what everyone had been thinking but no one had verbalized: they should draw lots to determine who would die so the others might live. Richard Parker, the seventeen-year-old cabin boy, lay semiconscious from drinking seawater. He never participated in the lottery that decided his fate. Dudley killed him with a penknife on the twentieth day. The three surviving men consumed Parker's body over four days before a German ship rescued them. When they returned to England in 1884, authorities charged them with murder. The defense argued necessity. The prosecution argued that necessity doesn't suspend the fundamental prohibition against killing and eating other humans. The jury convicted them. The court sentenced them to death, then commuted it to six months. This legal hairsplitting—we understand why you did it, we might have done the same, but we absolutely cannot permit it—reveals the core psychic crisis that survival cannibalism creates. We recognize the logic while recoiling from the precedent.

What makes survival cannibalism intellectually distinct from ritual or gustatory variants isn't the absence of choice—that's the comfortable fiction we tell ourselves. It's the presence of a specific cognitive architecture: the calculated decision tree that weighs continuation of life against the transgression required to achieve it, made under conditions of metabolic desperation that distort normal decision-making capacity. The human brain running on depleted glucose stores doesn't function like the brain considering hypotheticals in comfort. Starvation produces measurable cognitive impairment within days. After two weeks without food, executive function deteriorates. After three weeks, the body begins consuming its own organs. The decision to eat human flesh under these conditions happens in a neurological state so altered from baseline that calling it "choice" in any meaningful sense becomes philosophically questionable. Yet we insist on treating it as a moral decision rather than a biological inevitability because the alternative—accepting that extreme conditions reduce humans to survival machines—threatens our self-conception as rational agents in control of our ethical parameters.

The Physiology of Desperation

Your body doesn't care about taboos. When caloric intake drops below maintenance levels, metabolic processes shift into conservation mode. The liver exhausts its glycogen stores within twenty-four hours. Then fat reserves oxidize. This produces ketone bodies that the brain uses for fuel, but ketosis brings mental fog, irritability, and difficulty concentrating. After fat stores deplete—which happens faster than most people realize, particularly in cold environments where thermoregulation demands enormous energy—the body begins catabolizing muscle tissue. Not just skeletal muscle; cardiac muscle. The heart literally digests itself to keep the brain functioning. This is what the men aboard the *Méduse* experienced in 1816 when their frigate ran aground off Mauritania. The officers commandeered the lifeboats, abandoning 146 soldiers and sailors on a makeshift raft with minimal provisions. After three days, survivors began drinking urine. After six days, they began eating the dead, starting with those who'd died from exposure and dehydration. By the time rescue arrived on the thirteenth day, fifteen men remained alive. The physician aboard, Jean Baptiste Henri Savigny, later documented the progression in clinical detail: how the first transgression created psychological permission for subsequent ones, how survivors developed systematic methods for butchering and preservation, how the line between "already dead" and "might die soon anyway" eroded under sustained metabolic crisis.

The metabolic mathematics are straightforward. An adult male burns approximately 1,800 to 2,500 calories daily at rest, more with activity or cold exposure. Human muscle tissue provides roughly 600 calories per pound. A 170-pound human body contains approximately 60 pounds of skeletal muscle—theoretically, 36,000 calories if completely consumed, which it never is due to inedible portions and preparation losses. This represents perhaps two weeks of survival for a single person, less if shared among a group. These calculations matter because they expose the temporal limitation of cannibalism as a survival strategy. It's a bridge, not a destination. The survivors of the Donner Party understood this. Trapped in the Sierra Nevada during the winter of 1846-47, they consumed the dead over a period of months, but the cannibalism alone didn't save them—it extended their viability until rescue parties could reach them. Without external intervention, cannibalism merely postpones the inevitable while creating additional moral debt. The Uruguayan rugby team stranded in the Andes after their plane crashed in 1972 faced this recognition: eating their dead teammates bought time, but time wasn't the solution. They still needed rescue, still required someone from the functioning world to reach them.

Decision Architecture Under Duress

The sequence of psychological concessions follows a predictable pattern across documented cases. First comes the discussion of whether to eat those who've already died. This conversation typically begins obliquely, with hypotheticals and abstractions, before crystallizing into specific proposals. The framers of these discussions universally invoke necessity, universalize the situation—"anyone would," "we must," "there's no alternative." This linguistic construction attempts to distribute moral responsibility across the group and across humanity itself, making the transgression collective rather than individual. Once the group consumes already-deceased individuals, a threshold breaks, and the second transgression— determining who dies next when deaths from natural causes haven't occurred quickly enough—requires a different justification architecture. Here, the calculations become explicitly utilitarian. Who is already closest to death? Who contributes least to collective survival odds? Who has no dependents waiting for them? The crew of the *Essex*, rammed and sunk by a sperm whale in 1820, drew lots to determine who would be killed for food. They structured it as fair randomization, democracy applied to mortality. But Chase, the first mate who documented the ordeal, noted that the dying were excluded from the lottery because death's imminence made them "naturally" available. This created a perverse incentive: appearing too weak meant exclusion from the lottery's protection while guaranteeing consumption. The logical endpoint—accelerating someone's death to avoid the lottery's verdict—went unacknowledged in written accounts but remains mathematically implicit in the timeline.

What survivors report afterward isn't guilt over the act itself, which most describe as dissociated, mechanical, and necessary. The

31

persistent psychological damage comes from the memory of decision clarity. Multiple survivors across different disasters describe experiencing unusual mental lucidity in the hours surrounding cannibalistic consumption, a sharpness of thought that felt foreign and disturbing. The brain, receiving nutrition after extended deprivation, briefly operates at enhanced capacity—right when you're violating the deepest cultural prohibition. This neurological irony creates lasting trauma: the moments when they felt most clear-headed were the moments they were eating other humans. That clarity becomes contaminated in retrospect. Some survivors report decades-long aversions to meat generally, not because it reminds them of human flesh but because the act of tearing meat with teeth triggers visceral memory of that unwanted lucidity. The psychologist embedded with the Andes survivors documented this extensively: several men who'd found the strength to hike out for rescue after consuming their friends later developed eating disorders, chronic nausea, or eliminated meat from their diets despite acknowledging the nutritional necessity that saved them.

The Legal Fictions We Maintain

Every legal system maintains a contradiction regarding survival cannibalism. Murder statutes permit no defense of necessity—you cannot kill an innocent person to save yourself or others, full stop. Yet consumption of those already dead receives tacit permission, provided you didn't cause the death. This creates an impossible position: cannibalism is legally tolerable only if someone died conveniently without your intervention. The moment you acknowledge that waiting for natural death might take too long to serve its survival function, the entire legal framework collapses into incoherence. British Admiralty courts grappled with this after the *Francis Spaight* survivors in 1835 drew lots to determine who'd be killed. The court ruled that drawing lots didn't convert murder into something else. The necessity defense failed. Yet private correspondence among the judges revealed their recognition that refusing the defense created a perverse alternative: better to secretly kill the weakest and claim natural death than to use randomization, since transparency guaranteed conviction while deception might not. The law was incentivizing dishonesty about survival decisions made under duress.

Modern jurisprudence hasn't resolved this tension; it's simply stopped prosecuting. When the Andes survivors returned to civilization in 1972, Uruguayan authorities conducted investigations but filed no charges. The decision was political pragmatism dressed as mercy, but it established an operational precedent: survival cannibalism will be documented, deplored, and ultimately excused through bureaucratic paralysis rather than formal exoneration. This leaves victims' families in legal limbo. They cannot pursue wrongful death claims because no crime was officially committed. They cannot claim their relative died of natural causes because the body was consumed. The death certificate lists "accident/misadventure" or remains incomplete. This administrative ambiguity protects survivors from prosecution while denying families the closure that formal legal proceedings, however painful, might provide. We've created a system that acknowledges survival cannibalism without authorizing it, that understands its logic without legitimating it, that excuses perpetrators while abandoning victims to categorical uncertainty.

Preparation Methods and Cognitive Dissociation

The technical aspects of post-mortem processing reveal something about human psychology under extreme stress: the retreat into procedure as a defense against emotional reality. Survivors consistently report approaching butchery with clinical detachment, focusing on mechanical efficiency rather than acknowledging what they're processing. The Andes survivors developed systematic methods—using glass shards from the fuselage to cut, arranging meat on aluminum sheets in the sun to dry, storing portions in snow banks to preserve them. This procedural approach served dual purposes: practical preservation of scarce resources and psychological protection through task focus. If you're concentrating on cutting properly, managing temperatures, and preventing spoilage, you're not confronting the fact that you're preparing your friend's body for consumption. Multiple survivors described the work as eerily similar to field-dressing game animals, which several had done before. The brain, desperate for familiar frameworks when confronting the unfamiliar, mapped available cognitive schemas onto unprecedented situations.

The evolution from initial revulsion to routine consumption typically spans three to five days. First consumption produces near-universal nausea, vomiting, and psychological resistance. Second consumption goes slightly easier—the body recognizes nutrition even as the mind recoils. By the third or fourth time, survivors report the act becoming mechanical, stripped of emotional valence. This isn't desensitization in the clinical sense; it's compartmentalization. The part of consciousness that experiences disgust gets walled off from the part executing survival behaviors. Some survivors describe watching themselves eat as though observing someone else, a dissociative state that protected sanity during the act but complicated reintegration afterward. When dissociation becomes your survival strategy, you create internal divisions that don't heal easily. Years later, survivors report still experiencing that split—the observer and the actor existing simultaneously, unable to fully reunite into coherent selfhood.

The Hierarchy of Transgression

Not all survival cannibalism weighs equally on the participants' psyches. Consuming someone who died from exposure, injury, or illness produces less lasting trauma than consuming someone killed specifically for food. This moral gradient appears consistently across survivor accounts regardless of culture, religion, or era. The psychological distinction rests on agency: eating someone already dead feels like resourceful opportunism; killing someone to eat them feels like murder, regardless of lottery systems or group consensus. Even when survivors participate in drawing lots and accept the theoretical legitimacy of the process, those who actually performed the killing carry a disproportionate psychological burden. Thomas Dudley, who killed Richard Parker aboard the *Mignonette*, never fully recovered. He maintained that necessity justified his actions, yet his personal correspondence reveals persistent nightmares, religious obsession, and what we'd now recognize as post-traumatic stress disorder. The act of killing corrupted him in ways that simply consuming flesh did not corrupt the other survivors.

This hierarchy extends to relationship proximity. Eating strangers produces less trauma than eating acquaintances, which produces less trauma than eating friends or family. The Andes survivors existed in a uniquely torturous position—they were teammates, friends, and some were relatives. They knew favorite foods, inside jokes, and family histories. This intimacy meant that processing bodies required not just overcoming the prohibition against cannibalism but betraying a personal relationship. Several survivors described having to prepare close friends' bodies while actively suppressing specific memories of those individuals. One reported that he couldn't look at faces during butchery because recognition made the work impossible. He focused on limbs, torso sections, and anatomical abstractions rather than personal wholes. Years later, in therapy, he described this as murder by redefinition—treating people as parts rather than integrated beings. The intellectual violence of that reframing caused more lasting damage than the physical act of consumption.

The aftermath testimony reveals an uncomfortable truth: humans adapt to survival cannibalism with disturbing efficiency when metabolic necessity overrides cultural prohibition. The real psychological catastrophe comes later, in safety, when the biological imperative lifts and moral accounting begins. Every survivor interviewed long-term describes a bifurcated existence—the person who did what was necessary to live, and the person who must now live with what was done. These aren't reconcilable identities. They coexist in permanent tension, neither fully dominant nor fully suppressed. We prefer redemption narratives where survivors heal, integrate their experiences, and move forward. But the honest accounts suggest something bleaker: you don't recover from survival cannibalism. You accommodate it. You build a life that contains that history without being consumed by it, but it never becomes acceptable, never transforms into just another hardship overcome. It remains a violation of the self that preserves the self, a paradox with no resolution except continuation.

The Conspiracy of Silence

What doesn't get discussed in polite retrospectives: the survivors who didn't make it out weren't just unlucky. In several documented cases, those who died later in the ordeal—after cannibalism had already begun—were metabolically disadvantaged by receiving smaller portions than stronger members of the group. The Andes survivors maintained that distribution was equal, but nutritional analysis of the timeline suggests otherwise. Those who ultimately perished had been weakening faster, which meant they worked less, which created implicit justification for reduced rations, which accelerated their decline. No one openly advocated unequal distribution. It emerged through unstated collective calculus: the strong have better odds of hiking out for rescue; therefore, preserving the strong maximizes everyone's theoretical survival chances, including the weak, who benefit from potential rescue. This logic is impeccable and monstrous. It converts people into probability calculations. The man who receives less flesh because he's less likely to be useful has been murdered by an actuarial table rather than a knife, but he's been murdered nonetheless.

Survivor accounts never acknowledge this directly. They describe deaths from injuries, from altitude sickness, and from giving up psychologically. They don't explain the metabolic mathematics that made those deaths inevitable once resource distribution became implicitly tiered. The conspiracy of silence protects everyone—the survivors from accusation, the families from unbearable specifics, society from confronting what utilitarianism actually looks like when implemented by freezing, starving humans with no philosophical training but plenty of survival instinct. We accept the sanitized version because the accurate version indicts not just the survivors but the entire framework of rational ethics we've built. If these people— ordinary humans in extraordinary circumstances—couldn't maintain egalitarian principles under pressure, what does that suggest about the principles themselves? Perhaps they're luxury beliefs that evaporate under the heat of actual crisis. Or maybe they're genuine aspirations that require surplus resources to implement. Either conclusion disturbs our self-conception.

The documentary record shows careful curation. Written accounts from survivors of the *Méduse* raft were edited before publication to remove passages describing how the strongest survivors pushed weaker members overboard during the night to conserve resources. The censored sections surfaced centuries later in private archives. Modern readers expressed shock at the deletions, but the original editors understood something we've forgotten: the complete truth doesn't serve communal healing. Partial truth allows reintegration. The Andes survivors collectively agreed never to reveal certain specifics—who was consumed when, which bodies were most extensively utilized, what exactly happened during the worst nights. This wasn't a cover-up. It was recognition that some knowledge only generates suffering without producing insight. The families who learned their sons' bodies provided sustenance could make peace with that necessity. The families who learned their sons' bodies were consumed down to the marrow, while others were barely touched, would have been destroyed by the implication. Measured dishonesty became an act of mercy.

But this creates historiographic problems. How do we analyze survival cannibalism rigorously when primary sources have been deliberately sanitized? How do we extract ethical principles from incomplete data sets? The academic literature dances around this, treating survivor testimony as sacred text rather than interested narration. No one wants to be the scholar who calls victims liars, even when the lies serve obvious psychological purposes. So we end up with a scholarship that takes selective memory as fact, that treats collective narratives as objective accounts, that mistakes what survivors need to believe happened for what actually occurred. The result is a body of work on survival cannibalism that confirms our preferences rather than challenges our assumptions. We learn that humans maintain their essential decency under duress. We know that desperate circumstances don't erase moral reasoning. We understand that cooperation and fairness persist even in extremity. Maybe that's all true. Or perhaps it's comforting fiction built on partial testimony from people who need to believe their actions were justifiable. The difference matters.

The few researchers who've pushed for complete disclosure have been professionally marginalized, accused of sensationalism or victim exploitation. But their work reveals patterns that sanitized accounts obscure. Hierarchies emerge quickly in survival situations. Leadership structures that were notional become rigidly enforced. Those with survival skills gain disproportionate influence. And crucially—most crucially—the people who make it out are the people who were willing to do what was necessary. That's selection bias masquerading as moral victory. We interview the survivors and conclude that humans can maintain ethics under pressure. But we're not interviewing the people who maintained ethics and died because of it. We're interviewing the people who survived, which tells us nothing about ethics and everything about effectiveness.

Chapter 4: The Sacred and the Sinister: Religious Cannibalism Explored

The Eucharist terrifies no one. Every Sunday, millions of Christians consume what they believe to be the literal body and blood of Christ—transubstantiation, not metaphor, according to Catholic doctrine—and walk out of church without triggering a single moral alarm. This ought to disturb us more than it does. Not because communion is genuinely cannibalistic in practice, but because it reveals something we'd rather not acknowledge: the human mind possesses an extraordinary capacity to reconcile the consumption of divine flesh with moral righteousness when the proper theological scaffolding supports it. Strip away two thousand years of ecclesiastical authority, and what remains is a ritual that explicitly sacralizes anthropophagy, that makes the eating of God's incarnate form not just permissible but mandatory for salvation. The psychological architecture that makes this acceptable—that transforms cannibalism from abomination into sacrament—deserves scrutiny we consistently refuse to provide. We've spent centuries insisting that "our" sacred consumption differs fundamentally from "their" primitive rituals, but the difference is ceremonial vocabulary, not underlying logic.

The Theological Machinery of Acceptable Consumption

When religious systems authorize cannibalism, they don't argue for its morality—they transcend the category of morality entirely. The Aghoris of Varanasi, the ascetic Shaivite sect that practices occasional consumption of human corpse flesh, don't defend the practice as ethical. They position it as a transgressive necessity, a deliberate violation of social law that demonstrates transcendence of dualistic thinking. An Aghori sadhu eating putrefied brain matter from a skull bowl at a cremation ground isn't making a nutritional choice or honoring the dead. He's performing a liturgy of radical non-dualism, insisting through the most visceral method available that categories like pure/impure, sacred/profane, permissible/forbidden are illusions binding ordinary consciousness. The theological sophistication here matches anything in Christian mysticism. Still, we can't examine it seriously without confronting an uncomfortable parallel: both systems use human flesh as technology for accessing divine reality. The Aghori explicitly rejects social norms; the Christian implicitly reinforces them. Yet both claim that consuming sanctified human tissue brings the practitioner closer to the ultimate truth.

This pattern repeats across religious traditions with variations in intensity but remarkable consistency in structure. The Vama Marga practitioners of tantric Buddhism in medieval Tibet reportedly consumed small amounts of human tissue from executed criminals during specific empowerment rituals—not as punishment for the dead or nutrition for the living, but as a charging mechanism for spiritual advancement. The flesh served as a conductor for transmitted realization from guru to initiate, its transgressive nature generating the psychological shock necessary to shatter conventional mental frameworks. These weren't savage tribes stumbling toward enlightenment through random taboo violation. These were sophisticated philosophical traditions with libraries, universities, and centuries of theoretical development, concluding after rigorous analysis that consuming human flesh under precise ceremonial conditions accelerated liberation from cyclic existence. When we dismiss such practices as primitive while defending communion as civilized, we're not making a theological argument. We're making a tribal one.

The anthropological records from Christian Ethiopia document something even more unsettling: the Tewahedo Orthodox Church's historical relationship with the Qemant people's Beta Israel traditions included documented disputes over whether certain healing rituals crossed into anthropophagic territory. Nineteenth-century missionary accounts—admittedly written by observers with their own biases—describe Ethiopian Christians accusing traditional practitioners of grinding human bone into medicinal powders. In contrast, the accused responded by pointing out that Christian consumption of Christ's body at every mass made the Catholics, in particular, poor judges of what constituted sacred versus profane consumption. Neither side was wrong. Both had constructed elaborate theological justifications for ingesting substances they classified as human in origin and divine in nature. The difference was geopolitical power, not moral clarity.

The Economics of Sacred Flesh

Religious cannibalism operates within exchange systems that expose the material basis of spiritual practice. The Hua people of Papua New Guinea's Eastern Highlands maintained, until Australian colonial intervention in the 1960s, an elaborate system of ritual cannibalism embedded in their understanding of "nu," a vital essence transmitted through consuming specific body parts of particular individuals under specific circumstances. But nu wasn't distributed equally. Adult males possessed potent nu; women and children had less. Enemy warriors killed in battle held nu that could be captured and converted to benefit the consumer's lineage. Dead relatives required consumption to prevent their nu from dissipating into waste. This created an entire economy of spiritual calories that paralleled, and sometimes superseded, ordinary food economics. Funeral feasts required precise calculation: which kin had the obligation to consume which portions, how much nu transfer was necessary to satisfy both the living's needs and the dead's proper transition, and whether there was excess that could be traded to neighboring clans for political advantage.

The materiality of this system refutes any notion that religious cannibalism exists purely in a symbolic register. The Hua weren't engaging in metaphor any more than a banker trading mortgage-backed securities is engaging in metaphor. They were manipulating a resource they considered real, measurable, and consequential. Western anthropologists initially dismissed nu as superstition, but that framing misses the functional point. Whether or not nu exists in physical fact, the belief in its existence generated real economic behavior with real social consequences. Families bankrupted themselves hosting funerary feasts because failing to consume enough nu-rich tissue endangered the lineage's future vitality. Young men sought to consume enemy warriors' organs to enhance their own combat effectiveness in subsequent raids. The system operated with such internal consistency that when Australian colonial authorities banned cannibalism, they inadvertently collapsed an entire invisible economy, triggering social dysfunction that took decades to stabilize because there was no equivalent substitute for nu-based exchange.

The Catholicism that replaced these practices brought its own economy of sacred consumption. The Eucharist doesn't just feed souls—it generates institutional power through controlled access to salvific grace. The priest alone can consecrate, can transform bread into flesh. This monopoly on transubstantiation creates dependency:

the faithful must return weekly, must submit to ecclesiastical authority, must acknowledge the Church's unique power to provide the consumed flesh of God. It's a brilliant system, unlike the Huas' nu, which theoretically any initiated adult could harvest through proper ritual and access to appropriate bodies. The Church centralized the production of sacred flesh under hierarchical control. The theological justification differs radically from Melanesian systems, but the structural function—using controlled access to consumable human/divine flesh to maintain social order and institutional power—operates identically. We don't call it economy because we've learned to use different vocabulary, but the confession booth and the communion rail serve the same social function as the Hua feast circle: regulating who receives spiritual nutrition, under what conditions, maintaining hierarchy through ceremonial distribution of substances classified as fundamentally different from ordinary food.

The Semiotics of Pollution and Purity

Religious cannibalism exists at the unstable boundary between the absolutely polluting and the supremely purifying. The Balinese corpse-eating rituals documented by Margaret Eisenstadt in the 1980s—practiced by certain Brahman priests who consumed tiny portions of cremated human ash mixed with holy water during specific purification ceremonies—demonstrate this paradox with remarkable clarity. The ash represented ultimate pollution: death itself, rendered into particulate form. Yet the ritual's purpose was purification, specifically the most extreme purification available to human practitioners. The priest consumed pollution to transcend pollution, ingested death to overcome death, and took the most contaminating substance imaginable into his body to demonstrate that purity and impurity were perceptual categories without ultimate reality. This isn't logical in the way we typically use that term. It's symbolic logic, operating through ritual grammar, that makes perfect sense within the system while appearing absurd from outside.

The theological gymnastics required to make this work reveal something about religious thought more broadly: the need for paradox at the system's core, for a contradiction so profound that resolving it requires transcendent consciousness. Christianity does this with the Trinity—three persons, one God, internally incoherent yet central to faith. Buddhism does it with emptiness that is simultaneously form. Hindu philosophy does it with the identity of Atman and Brahman despite their apparent distinction. Religious cannibalism literalizes this paradox by making the body simultaneously food and not-food, person and not-person, polluting substance and purifying sacrament. You can't halfheartedly consume human flesh while maintaining it's sacred. The act requires total commitment to a framework that ordinary logic rejects. That's precisely the point. The transgression itself becomes the gateway to transcendence, not despite its moral violence but because of it.

The medieval Christian mystics understood this better than modern theologians want to acknowledge. Catherine of Siena described her mystical experiences in explicitly cannibalistic terms: consuming Christ's flesh in vision, drinking from his wounds, experiencing spiritual union through ingestion of divine substance. Her confessors worried these visions were demonic precisely because they seemed to literalize the Eucharist beyond acceptable boundaries. Suppose the Mass makes consuming Christ's body sacred. What does it mean when a mystic reports doing so outside official channels, during private prayer, with visceral intensity that exceeds liturgical boundaries? The institutional Church couldn't condemn her without undermining transubstantiation, couldn't endorse her without authorizing individual access to divine flesh that bypassed clerical mediation. They canonized her eventually, but the tension never resolved. Her mystical cannibalism remained simultaneously the height of devotion and perpetually suspect, too extreme and yet perfectly consistent with official doctrine. The contradiction wasn't an error in the system. It was the system working exactly as designed, generating a paradox that forced believers into permanent theological vertigo.

The Transmission Problem

Every religious tradition that incorporates cannibalism faces the same pedagogical crisis: how do you teach newcomers that the forbidden is mandatory, that disgust must transform into devotion, that the body's visceral rejection must be overridden by theological commitment? The Korowai people of West Papua solved this through gradual initiation. Children weren't brought to funerary feasts where deceased clan members were consumed until they'd undergone years of preparation, hearing stories that positioned the practice within complex kinship obligations and cosmological necessity. By the time a

42

child witnessed their first consumption, it arrived embedded in such a thick narrative context that the physical act became almost secondary to its meaning. Almost. Former practitioners interviewed after conversion to Christianity consistently report that initial exposure produced profound nausea that took weeks or months to overcome, but that refusing participation would have meant social death, exclusion from adult status, and community recognition. The coercion wasn't physical—no one forced flesh down unwilling throats—but social, psychological, total.

Christianity uses different methods toward identical ends. Catholic children receive first communion around age seven, after months of catechism drilling the real presence doctrine into developing minds. The ceremony emphasizes beauty, solemnity, special clothing, family celebration—everything except the literal claim being made. By the time the child understands they've been taught they're consuming actual human flesh, they're so embedded in the practice and its social reinforcement that questioning it becomes nearly impossible. The genius of the system is its gradualism: the doctrine is too complex for young children to grasp fully, so by the time comprehension arrives, habit has already formed. This isn't an accident or pedagogical failure. It's sophisticated behavioral conditioning that would make Pavlov envious. You can't convince a rational adult with no prior exposure that eating God is sensible. You can convince a seven-year-old who trusts their parents and community, then rely on cognitive dissonance reduction to prevent later rejection of the practice once critical thinking develops.

The transmission problem becomes acute when systems encounter each other. When Spanish missionaries confronted Mesoamerican ritual cannibalism in the sixteenth century, they faced uncomfortable parallels between indigenous practices and their own Eucharistic theology. Some indigenous people, upon hearing transubstantiation explained, reportedly responded that their own rituals were remarkably similar—they too consumed flesh to honor gods, to maintain cosmic order, to create communion between human and divine. The Spanish insisted the differences were absolute, but their arguments relied on assertions of unique divine authorization rather than structural distinction. Both systems claimed that proper consumption of human flesh brought practitioners closer to ultimate reality. Both demanded the practice as a religious obligation—both punished refusal. The critical difference was which God authorized the consumption, not whether the consumption itself was sacred or profane. This recognition never made it into official histories because it threatened the entire colonial justification. If Aztec ritual cannibalism and Catholic communion operated on parallel theological logic, then the moral authority for condemning one while mandating the other collapsed into cultural preference rather than universal truth.

The Post-Religious Hangover

Societies that abandoned religious cannibalism face persistent psychological residue that manifests in unexpected ways. Japan's relationship with Christianity includes a centuries-long period during which converts practiced in secret, modifying rituals to avoid detection. The kakure kirishitan—hidden Christians—of Nagasaki Prefecture maintained Eucharistic ceremonies using substitutes when priests weren't available, eventually developing entirely separate theological interpretations that drifted so far from orthodoxy that when religious freedom arrived in the nineteenth century, most refused reconciliation with Rome. But their ritual preserved the central act: consuming something understood as Christ's flesh, performing the cannibalistic sacrament in basements and forests under penalty of death. When anthropologists studied these communities in the 1950s, descendants who no longer believed the theology still practiced modified versions of the ritual, consuming rice balls blessed with prayers whose meanings they'd forgotten, performing motions inherited through generations but disconnected from the original theological framework. The cannibalistic impulse had survived the death of its justification, becoming cultural muscle memory.

Modern secular societies that developed from Christian foundations show similar patterns. The persistence of phrases like "you are what you eat" or the visceral reaction against cannibalism that exceeds reactions to other violations suggests internalized theological conditioning operating beneath conscious awareness. We don't just think cannibalism is wrong—we experience it as categorically different from other harms, uniquely polluting, a contact with a boundary that must never be crossed. This isn't universal human nature. It's the psychological aftermath of religious systems that made consuming sanctified flesh mandatory while condemning all other anthropophagy as absolute evil. The contradiction generated intense anxiety around ingestion, around bodily boundaries, around the transformation of substance that eating represents. Contemporary Western eating disorders, with their obsessive focus on controlling what enters the body and their moralization of food categories into pure and impure, clean and contaminating, may represent secularized versions of theological anxiety originally generated by the sacred cannibalism/profane cannibalism binary.

The pharmaceutical industry's use of human-derived materials reveals this anxiety in commercial form. Premarin, the hormone replacement therapy, was sourced from pregnant mares' urine for decades without significant protest. But when biotech companies proposed using cultured human tissue for medical applications—lab-grown skin, engineered organs, cellular therapies—public resistance exploded despite the obvious medical benefits and ethical superiority to animal-sourced materials. The objection wasn't rational; it was visceral, ancient, and theological. Using human tissue, even tissue grown in controlled laboratory conditions from voluntarily donated cells, triggered the cannibalism taboo that centuries of Christian conditioning had embedded into Western consciousness. We've removed the religious framework, but the psychological architecture it built remains operational, generating disgust toward practices our secular ethics struggle to condemn. This is what religious cannibalism's legacy looks like: a revulsion so profound it survives the death of its justification and continues shaping behavior in societies that have forgotten why they believe what they believe about the fundamental wrongness of consuming human substance.

The sacred and the sinister occupy the same territory in religious cannibalism because religion itself operates through the transformation of categories that ordinary thought treats as stable. What begins as ultimate transgression becomes ultimate devotion through liturgical alchemy that changes nothing material about the act while changing everything about its meaning. This isn't unique to cannibalism—sacrifice, martyrdom, ascetic self-harm all follow identical logic—but anthropophagy's intensity makes the transformation visible in ways other practices obscure. When you make eating human flesh not just acceptable but mandatory for salvation, you've revealed the core mechanism of religious authority:

the power to redefine reality itself through collective agreement to see the same object simultaneously as what it materially is and what the system insists it means. The flesh is bread. The bread is flesh. Both statements are true. Neither statement is true. The contradiction is the point. And every believer who consumes it reinforces the system's authority to dictate meaning despite material fact, to maintain that the most forbidden act becomes the most sacred when performed under proper theological authorization. That power—to make the impossible mandatory, the disgusting holy, the cannibalistic divine—is what religious systems actually trade in. Everything else is commentary.

Chapter 5: Cultural Narratives: Cannibalism in Myth and Folklore

The Brothers Grimm didn't flinch. When they collected *Hänsel und Gretel* in 1812, they preserved the witch's explicit intention: fatten the children, roast them, eat them. Victorian translators later softened this, turning cannibalism into vague menace, but the original German makes the culinary objective clear. The witch wasn't metaphorically hungry for innocence—she was literally preparing to consume children as food. This bothers us less than it should. We've domesticated this story into children's entertainment, complete with gingerbread houses and sing-along cartoon adaptations, while conveniently forgetting that we're teaching toddlers about anthropophagic predation disguised as grandmotherly hospitality. The narrative architecture of the tale— stranger danger, resource scarcity driving parental abandonment, cannibalism as literalized evil—survived for centuries because it encoded real anxieties about famine, infanticide, and what hunger makes people capable of. But we've filed the story under "fantasy" and stopped examining what made it culturally necessary to tell.

Folklore operates as collective memory encoded in narrative form. When cannibalism appears in these stories—and it seems constantly, across every culture that developed oral tradition—it's not random shock value. It's the cultural processing of actual practice, actual fear, or actual transgression preserved in story form because direct historical documentation was unavailable or unbearable. The Japanese *yamauba* tales depict mountain-dwelling crones who lure travelers with hospitality before consuming them, a narrative pattern that maps suspiciously well to historical accounts of oyasute—the practice of abandoning elderly relatives in remote mountain locations during famine. The stories let communities discuss infanticide, geronticide, and cannibalism while maintaining plausible deniability. They weren't admitting these practices occurred; they were just telling cautionary tales about demons. This narrative laundering allowed communities to preserve the cultural memory of transgressive behavior without claiming direct historical culpability. The folklore becomes an admission and a denial simultaneously.

Narrative Structures as Moral Processing Systems

The cannibal figure in folklore follows recognizable typologies that reveal what each culture finds specifically terrifying about anthropophagy. The *wendigo* of Algonquian tradition embodies transformation cannibalism—the idea that consuming human flesh doesn't just violate taboo but fundamentally changes the consumer's nature, creating an insatiable monster that was once human but can never return. This narrative architecture appears wherever communities faced a genuine risk of survival cannibalism during harsh winters. The wendigo stories didn't just discourage the practice; they created a theological framework where even survival-driven consumption resulted in permanent spiritual contamination. You might live through the winter by eating your family, but you'd live as something other than human. The narrative made survival cannibalism literally worse than death.

Compare this to the ogre traditions of European folklore—Bluebeard, the giant in *Jack and the Beanstalk*, the troll under the bridge. These figures are externally monstrous, clearly Other, marked by their anthropophagy as existing outside humanity from the start. Their dietary practices do not transform them; their cannibalism simply reveals their inherent monstrosity. This reflects a different cultural anxiety: not that we might become cannibals, but that cannibals exist among us disguised as civilized people. The narrative warning shifts from "don't do this" to "be vigilant about who you trust." When Red Riding Hood discovers the wolf wearing her grandmother's clothing, the horror isn't transformation—it's recognition. The monster was always there, just wearing better camouflage. These European narratives emerged from societies with sufficient food security that survival cannibalism wasn't the primary threat, but stranger danger and predatory outsiders absolutely were.

The distinction between these narrative approaches maps to material conditions with uncomfortable precision. Societies facing regular subsistence crises developed transformation narratives that warned against practices their members might actually resort to. Societies with relative abundance developed infiltration narratives about external threats disguised as neighbors. Both systems use cannibalism as the ultimate signifier of evil, but they're encoding different fears and managing various risks. Neither tradition admits this openly. Both hide their pragmatic social-control function behind entertainment value and supernatural threat. The folklore works precisely because it operates below conscious analysis, installing behavioral guardrails while maintaining the fiction of mere storytelling.

The Trickster's Appetite: Transgression as Narrative Technology

Then there's the third category, the one that troubles easy analysis: the cannibal as trickster figure, consumer of human flesh who generates humor rather than horror. Polynesian oral traditions include Kae, who murders and eats Tinirau's pet whale, then lies about it with such creative audacity that the story becomes a comedy about transgression rather than a condemnation of it. West African Anansi stories occasionally feature anthropophagic episodes played for laughs, with the spider-trickster eating rivals or annoying relatives in ways that generate audience delight rather than revulsion. These narratives violate Western assumptions about how cannibalism functions symbolically. They're not encoding survival fears or warning against predators. They're doing something more complex: using anthropophagy as the ultimate transgression that proves the trickster's boundary-dissolving power.

The anthropologist Claude Lévi-Strauss spent decades trying to make trickster figures fit structural models, ultimately concluding they resist systematic analysis because they exist precisely to violate systematic categorization. The cannibal-trickster embraces this function. By consuming human flesh playfully, manipulatively, without the excuse of hunger or the pretense of ritual significance, these figures demonstrate that no rule is absolute, no taboo is universal, and no moral boundary prevents creative reinterpretation. This creates profound discomfort for audiences expecting folklore to reinforce social order. Instead, these stories suggest that social order itself might be arbitrary, that the most fundamental prohibitions might be situationally negotiable, that the universe doesn't particularly care which behavioral codes humans invent to organize themselves. The laughter these stories generate isn't comfortable—it's the nervous laughter of recognizing an uncomfortable truth you'd rather not examine.

Pacific Islander traditions developed particularly sophisticated versions of this narrative technology because they emerged from cultures where actual ritual anthropophagy existed within living memory. The stories couldn't simply demonize cannibalism without demonizing ancestors who practiced it. They couldn't completely normalize it without violating contemporary taboos that had emerged post-contact. The trickster cannibal solved this problem by existing outside normal moral evaluation. Kae's crime isn't that he ate flesh—it's that he lied about it poorly enough to get caught. The narrative focuses on deception and consequence rather than the act itself, allowing communities to discuss anthropophagy while maintaining ambiguity about whether it's fundamentally wrong or just socially impractical. This sophisticated moral ambiguity vanishes entirely in Western retellings, which insist on flattening complex ethical terrain into simple good-versus-evil binaries.

Fairy Tale Cannibalism and the Hidden History of Famine

The prevalence of cannibalism in European fairy tales reveals historical trauma that academic historians have spent centuries trying to explain away. *The Juniper Tree*, collected by the Grimm brothers, features a stepmother who murders her stepson, chops him into pieces, cooks him in stew, and serves him to his father. *The Children and the Ogre* involves explicit butchery preparation of kidnapped children. *The Story of the Youth Who Went Forth to Learn What Fear Was* includes an attempted roasting of the protagonist by hungry demons. The sheer frequency of these motifs, combined with their specific culinary detail—the cutting, the cooking methods, the serving techniques— suggests these aren't abstract metaphors. They're distorted memories of actual famine cannibalism encoded into oral tradition and sanitized through supernatural framing.

Documentary evidence supports this reading. The Great Famine of 1315-1317 killed millions across Europe and generated scattered chronicles describing parents eating children, though most such accounts come from monastic sources with questionable reliability. But the folklore that emerges during and immediately after this period shows a marked increase in cannibalistic themes, particularly involving children as victims and familial relationships as cover for predation. The narrative pattern isn't coincidental. Communities that couldn't openly discuss what happened during the famine—the social trust that shattered, the familial bonds that proved less durable than hunger— encoded these experiences in fantastical stories that could be told without triggering community fragmentation. The witch in the forest becomes a safe displacement for the neighbor who did something unspeakable when the grain stores ran empty. The evil stepmother becomes a narrative container for maternal rejection that communities couldn't acknowledge directly without destroying the kinship structures on which survival depended.

Modern sanitization of these tales—Disney's versions, children's book adaptations, theme park attractions—represents historical amnesia in action. We've extracted the entertainment value while discarding the cultural memory they encoded. The stories persist because they're good narratives with clear moral lessons about stranger danger and familial betrayal. But we've lost their function as collective trauma processing, as ritualized acknowledgment that yes, this happened, and yes, we survived it, and yes, we need to remember so it doesn't happen again. When we read *Hänsel und Gretel* to children now, we're teaching them about fictional witches while erasing the actual famine practices that generated the tale. The cultural forgetting is deliberate. We'd rather believe our ancestors never faced choices that would make us become the monsters in cautionary tales.

Colonial Projection and the Cannibal Savage Myth

Then, European colonialism weaponized the cannibal narrative entirely. Suddenly, folklore about man-eating Others stopped being about internal community threats and became justification for external conquest. The Caribbean Kalinago people gave us the word "cannibal"—derived from a Spanish mishearing of their name—but the etymological root hardly matters because Columbus and his successors deployed the label strategically regardless of accuracy. Declaring a population cannibalistic transformed them from potential trading partners into subhuman savages requiring salvation through subjugation. The legal framework of the era explicitly permitted the enslavement of cannibals as a protective measure. The narrative convenience of this should be obvious. Every resistance to colonial expansion could be reframed as evidence of savage nature, and anthropophagy served as the ultimate proof of savage nature, so any population resisting colonization must be cannibalistic. The circular logic required no actual evidence.

Missionaries generated most of the cannibal accusations, and their accounts follow suspicious patterns. They describe anthropophagic practices in lurid detail that reads less like ethnographic observation and more like pornographic fascination with transgression. They rarely provide verifiable witnesses beyond themselves. They frequently describe cannibalism in communities that archeological evidence shows had adequate food resources, eliminating survival necessity as motivation. And they often describe practices that make no practical sense—consuming enemies specifically to demonstrate contempt, or eating portions of bodies while burying others, or conducting multi-day ceremonies before consumption that would render flesh unsafe to eat. These narrative inconsistencies suggest invention rather than documentation.

The mythology these colonial sources created—the cannibal savage, perpetually hungry for human flesh, culturally predisposed to anthropophagy through moral deficiency—became embedded in Western folklore to the point that it still structures contemporary imagination. Tribal societies in adventure fiction routinely feature cannibalistic threats regardless of historical accuracy. The visual shorthand for primitive danger remains the cooking pot with bones sticking out. The narrative assumption that cannibalism indexes civilizational failure or cultural backwardness persists despite anthropological evidence that ritualized anthropophagy correlated with sophisticated social structures, not simple ones. We've built an entire folklore system on colonial propaganda, mistaken it for historical reality, and let it shape our understanding of cultural difference. The stories we tell about cannibals reveal less about practices in other cultures than about the psychological machinery we use to position ourselves as morally superior to populations we've systematically dispossessed.

Contemporary Urban Legends and the Persistence of Cannibalistic Anxiety

The Kentucky Fried Rat legend emerged in the 1970s—a customer bites into what they believe is chicken, discovers it's a battered and fried rat, and suffers trauma requiring hospitalization. The story spread nationwide despite never being verified, spawning variations where the victim receives massive legal settlements, or dies from shock, or discovers the contamination came from human fingers accidentally ground into meat processing. These urban legends represent cannibalism anxiety adapted to industrial food production. We've lost the ability to verify what we're eating because supply chains have become so complex that no consumer can trace the origin of the sources. The cannibal folklore adapts accordingly: the threat isn't the neighbor who might eat you during famine, it's the corporate system that might be feeding you human remains without disclosure or consent. The fundamental fear remains unchanged—involuntary consumption of human tissue—but the threat vector has shifted from individual predators to institutional negligence.

The persistence of these narratives reveals something about contemporary psychology that bears examination. We live in an era of unprecedented food abundance, at least in industrialized nations. Survival cannibalism represents functionally zero risk for most people reading this. Ritual anthropophagy has been successfully suppressed globally outside extremely isolated populations. Yet cannibalism remains a go-to horror element in fiction, urban legends, and moral panic narratives. Why? Because the taboo's strength hasn't diminished with the practice's frequency. If anything, the absence of real cannibalism in daily life has strengthened its symbolic power. It's become the ultimate transgression precisely because it's completely divorced from practical necessity. When we use cannibalism in contemporary horror—*The Silence of the Lambs*, *The Road*, *The Walking Dead*—we're not processing actual anthropophagic threats. We're using the most powerful symbol of dehumanization available to explore anxieties about entirely different social breakdowns: the collapse of empathy, the failure of institutions, the reduction of humans to resources.

The final twist in contemporary cannibal folklore involves the recycling of colonial-era myths as ironic distance entertainment. The "Cannibal Holocaust" genre of exploitation films, the "tribal" themed Halloween costumes complete with bones and cooking pots, the tiki bar aesthetic that treats anthropophagy as kitschy fun—these represent colonial propaganda so thoroughly absorbed that it's become nostalgic pop culture. We've moved from using cannibal narratives to justify conquest to using them to signal cultural sophistication through knowing reference. The underlying racism and historical violence that generated these images gets aestheticized away. We're performing appreciation of vintage colonialism without admitting that's what we're doing. The folklore has outlived its original function and found new life as content divorced from context, which might be the most troubling transformation of all.

The Fairy Tale Industrial Complex and Narrative Domestication

Disney's 1937 *Snow White* excised the cannibal Queen entirely. In the Grimm version, the Queen orders the huntsman to return with Snow White's lungs and liver as proof of death—then eats what she believes are those organs, boiled and salted. The film replaced this with a decorative heart in a jewelry box, sanitizing anthropophagy into a mere murder plot. This wasn't careless adaptation. It was a systematic removal of elements that complicated the simple villain narrative Disney's formula required. The Queen eating Snow White's internal organs makes her hungry in a way that reveals something uncomfortably human about her jealousy. She doesn't just want Snow White dead—she wants to consume her, to literally incorporate the beauty she covets. That's a psychologically complex motivation that children's entertainment can't accommodate without raising questions parents don't want to answer.

The pattern repeats across every major fairy tale adaptation. The cannibalistic elements get surgically removed while the narrative scaffolding remains intact. We keep teaching these stories to children because they contain valuable lessons about resilience, cleverness, and moral clarity. But we've created a peculiar cultural situation where entire generations grow up knowing sanitized versions, then express shock when encountering the original texts in college literature courses. The professor assigns the Grimm tales, students discover the anthropophagy they were never told about, and suddenly, they're questioning what else was edited out of their childhood. This manufactured innocence serves a purpose—it allows parents and educators to use folklore's narrative power without confronting the historical trauma that generated it. But it also creates a population that has inherited story structures without understanding their foundations, memorized metaphors without grasping what they originally meant.

The commercial incentive for this sanitization is obvious: you can't sell merchandise based on stories that honestly depict parents eating children during famine. The gingerbread house can become a theme park attraction only after you've stripped away the historical context of infanticide and survival cannibalism. The witch can become a Halloween costume only after her original function—encoding community memories of what hunger made people capable of—has been completely obscured. We've built an entire entertainment industry on folklore we've systematically hollowed out. The stories remain structurally intact but functionally inverted: instead of processing cultural trauma, they now generate profit by presenting that trauma as fantasy safely divorced from reality.

Some scholars argue that this represents healthy evolution, that cultures should adapt folklore to contemporary values rather than preserving historical violence. But that argument assumes the violence was only historical. The material conditions that generated these stories—resource scarcity, social breakdown, the question of what humans become when survival requires abandoning civilized behavior—haven't vanished. They've just migrated to populations we've decided not to think about. The climate crisis promises to reintroduce precisely the famine conditions that generated cannibal folklore in the first place. When we teach children sanitized fairy tales now, we're not protecting their innocence. We're failing to prepare them for possibilities our ancestors understood well enough to encode in stories that survived centuries. The domestication of cannibal narratives represents optimism mistaken for wisdom—the belief that erasing frightening stories somehow prevents the conditions that made them necessary.

Chapter 6: The Cannibal in Literature: From Horror to Satire

Jonathan Swift wanted to make you uncomfortable. When he published *A Modest Proposal* in 1729, suggesting that Irish peasants sell their children as gourmet food for English landlords, he wasn't making a culinary recommendation. He was performing vivisection on economic policy using cannibalism as a scalpel. The essay's genius lies not in its shock value—though eighteenth-century readers were thoroughly shocked—but in its mathematical precision. Swift calculates the exact age at which children reach optimal market weight, estimates fair pricing per pound, projects revenue generation for desperate families, and presents these obscenities in the measured prose of economic treatises that proposed equally monstrous policies without metaphorical distance. The satire works because it forces readers to confront a question they'd rather avoid: what's the moral difference between literally eating the poor and creating conditions that consume them through starvation, disease, and exploitation? Swift understood something contemporary readers miss when they file his essay under "classic satire" without examining its teeth. He wasn't using cannibalism to critique unrelated economic injustice. He was arguing that extractive colonial economics *is* cannibalism, just conducted through rental agreements and grain export policies instead of cookpots.

Literary cannibalism functions differently than anthropological or historical accounts because it operates in a hypothetical space where readers can't dismiss the practice as belonging to distant cultures or extreme circumstances. The cannibal appears in your language, targeting your society, challenging your complacency. Writers deploy anthropophagy as a philosophical weapon precisely because it cannot be domesticated, because it resists casual consumption even when presented as fiction. This creates a unique analytical opportunity: literature reveals what cultures fear about cannibalism that they can't articulate directly, what philosophical problems the practice generates that historical documentation avoids addressing, and what happens when you use human consumption as a thought experiment rather than a material act. The cannibal in literature isn't documenting what happened. It's interrogating what might happen, what the implications are, what it means about us that we're capable of imagining it in such detail.

The Gothic Cannibal: Consumption as Class Warfare

Gothic literature discovered cannibalism's symbolic efficiency early and never let go. But Gothic writers weren't primarily interested in the act itself—they were mapping power relations through digestive metaphors. The vampire represents aristocratic parasitism, literally sustaining itself on peasant blood while claiming noble necessity. It's cannibalism sanitized through supernatural distance, but the class critique remains obvious enough that nineteenth-century readers recognized it immediately. The werewolf performs different work: it demonstrates how civilization's veneer fractures under specific provocations, how the gentleman transforms into a predator when the moon is right, and how social position provides no immunity from bestial hunger. These monsters externalize anxieties about who's consuming whom in industrial capitalism, where factory owners weren't literally eating workers but were absolutely consuming their bodies through dangerous conditions, exploitative hours, and wages insufficient for adequate nutrition.

What makes Gothic anthropophagy particularly insidious is its tendency to aestheticize consumption. Vampires in nineteenth-century literature are uniformly attractive, sophisticated, culturally refined—everything their victims aren't. This inverts the savage-cannibal narrative that European colonialism had been constructing. The Gothic vampire suggests that the real anthropophagic threat comes from the educated elite, not primitive Others. Count Dracula isn't a Fijian warrior or Amazon tribesman—he's European nobility with centuries of accumulated culture who nevertheless reduces humans to livestock. Bram Stoker's novel, published in 1897 during Britain's imperial zenith, presents an interesting paradox: British characters express horror at Dracula's predation while completely failing to recognize their own empire's extractive consumption of colonized peoples. The novel lets readers experience moral outrage at fictional vampirism while maintaining a comfortable distance from the actual economic exploitation that their society practiced systematically. This is Gothic cannibalism's duplicitous function—it creates cathartic horror that substitutes for recognition of real predation.

The werewolf tradition operates through different mechanics but reaches similar conclusions about class and consumption. Lycanthropy in European folklore consistently appears as a curse or infection, something that happens *to* people rather than something they choose. This narrative framing does crucial ideological work: it suggests that those who prey on their neighbors aren't morally culpable because transformation stripped away volition. The werewolf can't help its nature. This becomes particularly convenient when examining who becomes werewolves in traditional tales— predominantly lower-class males, agricultural laborers, and social marginals. The aristocracy in these stories never transforms. The pattern isn't subtle. It encodes anxieties about lower-class violence while providing an exculpatory framework that higher classes conveniently never require because they're apparently immune to bestial reversion. When Gothic literature finally subverts this with aristocratic werewolves in the twentieth century, it signals shifting anxiety about where predatory threat actually originates. The recognition that wealth and refinement don't prevent consumption of others—might actually enable it—represents Gothic cannibalism achieving genuine philosophical insight rather than just generating atmospheric dread.

Twentieth-Century Modernism: The Cannibal as Metaphysical Crisis

Then modernist literature stripped away Gothic ornamentation and examined cannibalism with surgical directness. Herman Melville's "Benito Cereno" doesn't feature literal anthropophagy. Still, its depiction of enslaved Africans terrorizing their former captors generated accusations of depicting Black cannibalism that Melville never explicitly included—readers projected it because nineteenth-century racial ideology couldn't imagine enslaved people asserting dominance without attributing monstrous appetites to them. But the more interesting modernist engagement comes from writers who used cannibalism to interrogate consciousness itself rather than social relations. Joseph Conrad's *Heart of Darkness* mentions indigenous cannibalism obliquely. Still, the novel's actual interest lies in Kurtz's descent into what Conrad frames as savage consumption—though what Kurtz actually consumed was colonial power, using Company resources to establish himself as god-tyrant. The cannibalism here is a metaphorical displacement of recognizing that European imperialism was consuming Africa industrially while projecting anthropophagic savagery onto the victims of that consumption.

William Faulkner approached the problem more directly in *Sanctuary*, where Temple Drake's rape gets described through the language of consumption and predation that stops just short of literal cannibalism. The violence is sexual, but the framing is digestive—Popeye "consuming" Temple, reducing her to an object of appetites she can't escape. Faulkner was writing during the Depression in the American South, where economic collapse had created conditions approaching the famine-cannibalism scenarios that European fairy tales encoded. His deployment of consumption metaphors wasn't decorative. It diagnosed a culture devouring itself through violence; it refused to acknowledge directly, preferring to locate monstrosity in individual psychopaths like Popeye rather than examining systemic predation that created conditions for such individuals to flourish. This represents modernist literature's key contribution to cannibal narratives: the recognition that metaphorical and literal consumption exist on a continuum rather than as discrete categories. Faulkner forces readers to ask whether there's a meaningful moral distinction between Popeye's violence and the economic violence that impoverished Temple's family, between individual predation and societal structures that normalize exploitation.

The French existentialists took this further. Jean-Paul Sartre's *Being and Nothingness* contains an extended meditation on consumption as an ontological category—not just eating food but the way consciousness "consumes" objects through perception and possession, the way relationships involve mutual consumption of the Other's freedom. Sartre wasn't writing about literal cannibalism, but his philosophical framework treats all human interaction as fundamentally digestive: we incorporate others into our projects, we reduce their subjectivity to objects of our purposes, we metabolize their existence into fuel for our becoming. This philosophical anthropophagy reaches disturbing conclusions: if consciousness operates through consumption, if selfhood requires incorporating and digesting otherness, then cannibalism isn't aberrant behavior—it's the logical endpoint of how consciousness functions. Every I-Thou relationship secretly wants to become I-It, and the final form of It-ness is the consumed object that no longer possesses independent existence. Existentialist philosophy gave literary cannibalism its most radical interpretation: not as social transgression but as ontological revelation.

Postmodern Satire: The Cannibal as Commodity

Postmodern literature discovered that you can't satirize cannibalism through shock anymore—readers had developed immunity through decades of Gothic excess and modernist transgression. So writers shifted strategy, treating anthropophagy as capitalism's honest expression rather than its violation. Bret Easton Ellis's *American Psycho* culminates in explicit cannibalism performed by protagonist Patrick Bateman. Still, the novel's actual obscenity isn't the consumption of murdered women—it's the recognition that Bateman's cannibalism differs only in degree, not kind, from the economic consumption that defines his entire existence as a Wall Street executive. He consumes women's bodies the same way he consumes designer products, restaurant experiences, cocaine, and his own carefully constructed identity. Ellis wasn't condemning individual psychosis. He was arguing that late capitalism creates subjects who experience everything, including other humans, as consumable resources whose only meaning derives from the consumption act.

This represents satire abandoning moral instruction entirely. Swift's *Modest Proposal* presumed readers would recognize the horror and reject the policy. Ellis presumes readers recognize the horror and participate anyway because contemporary capitalism provides no alternative framework for relation. You can't oppose cannibalism on moral grounds while supporting economic systems that treat human labor as a commodity input. The hypocrisy becomes unsustainable. So Bateman eats his victims literally while his colleagues eat them metaphorically through corporate restructuring, and the novel refuses to identify which form of consumption deserves greater moral condemnation. This is postmodern satire's distinctive move: it deploys cannibalism not as a shocking metaphor meant to generate reform but as an accurate description of how we already relate to each other, acknowledging that the revelation of this fact won't change behavior because changing behavior would require abandoning the entire economic structure that defines contemporary existence.

Chuck Palahniuk's work extends this strategy into even more provocative territory. *Fight Club* features a moment where the narrator discovers Tyler Durden has been manufacturing soap from human fat stolen from liposuction clinics, which he then sells back to wealthy consumers who don't realize they're incorporating human remains into daily hygiene rituals. This isn't metaphorical cannibalism—it's actual consumption of human body material, just processed through commodity form rather than the digestive system. The narrative treats this revelation with dark humor rather than moral outrage because the point isn't that Tyler committed some unique transgression. The fact is that consumer capitalism already involves consuming each other constantly through labor exploitation, resource extraction, and market relations that reduce humans to economic units. Tyler just made the process literally visceral. Palahniuk's satire operates by demonstrating that we're already cannibals who've convinced ourselves otherwise through sufficient processing and packaging. The soap is morally equivalent to the iPhone assembled by workers in conditions that constitute consumption of their bodies through sustained physical degradation. We just find one form of consumption more aesthetically acceptable than the other.

Horror Fiction: The Banality of Appetite

Contemporary horror fiction discovered something modernist and postmodern literature missed: actual cannibalism, described with clinical precision, becomes less disturbing than metaphorical treatment because it externalizes the threat. If the monster literally eats human flesh, readers can position themselves in opposition, can imagine fighting back, and can maintain psychological distance. But if consumption operates metaphorically—if the horror lies in recognizing we're all implicated—escape becomes impossible. Thomas Harris understood this perfectly when creating Hannibal Lecter. The character works not because he eats people (fictional cannibals had been doing that for centuries) but because he's cultured, intelligent, aesthetically refined—everything that's supposed to prevent cannibalism according to Enlightenment theories about civilization taming savage nature. Lecter demonstrates that education and culture don't oppose anthropophagic urges; they refine them, making consumption more deliberate and selective rather than eliminating the appetite.

What's genuinely disturbing about Harris's portrayal isn't the violence—it's Lecter's complete absence of cognitive dissonance. He doesn't wrestle with the moral implications of consuming humans. He doesn't require elaborate theological justification like religious cannibals or desperate necessity like survival cannibals. He simply recognizes that he finds certain people unworthy of existence and delicious when properly prepared, then acts on that recognition with the same casual competence someone might apply to preparing venison. This attitude terrifies readers more than any amount of gore because it suggests that cannibalism doesn't require insanity, doesn't require supernatural compulsion, doesn't require elaborate rationalization. It just involves appetite plus opportunity plus absence of concern for conventional morality. The horror lies in recognizing how thin the barriers actually are, how little psychological architecture separates Lecter from any other apex predator who's decided certain prey items are acceptable to consume.

Horror fiction's other major contribution involves examining cannibalism's aftermath—not the act itself but what it does to survivors. The genre developed a sophisticated interest in what happens psychologically after you've consumed human flesh, whether by choice or compulsion. Scott Smith's *The Ruins* traps characters in a situation where they must progressively amputate and potentially cannibalize each other to survive parasitic plants, but the novel's real horror emerges from characters' recognition that they're willing to do it, that survival instinct overrides moral prohibition more easily than anyone expected. The trauma isn't committing anthropophagy—it's discovering your own adaptability, your capacity to rationalize anything with sufficient pressure. This represents horror literature moving beyond simple transgression into genuine philosophical territory: the recognition that humans possess nearly infinite moral flexibility, that we'll construct elaborate justifications for whatever we need to do, that the principles we claim as absolute collapse rapidly under appropriate stress.

The Satirical Cannibal: Comedy as Philosophical Weapon

Then there's the tradition that treats cannibalism as darkly comedic, using humor not to defuse the horror but to intensify it through tonal dissonance. Roald Dahl's short stories frequently feature anthropophagy played for laughs—"Pig" ends with a vegetarian discovering he's about to be butchered and consumed by the hotel staff, "The Landlady" strongly implies the protagonist will become the latest addition to the landlady's collection of preserved young men. Dahl's genius lies in maintaining a cozy, conversational tone while describing circumstances that ought to generate terror. This creates a unique cognitive effect: readers recognize the horror, but the narrative voice refuses to validate that recognition, continues describing monstrous events in the same cheerful register you'd use for discussing pleasant weather. The tonal mismatch forces readers to confront their own reaction—why are we disturbed when the narrator isn't? What does it mean that cannibalism can be narrated casually? The comedy comes from recognition of absurdity, but the absurdity isn't the cannibalism itself—we expect that it deserves special narrative treatment.

Edward Gorey's illustrated works take this further by removing all psychological interiority. His characters experience elaborate deaths and implied consumption with complete affective flatness, expressing neither fear nor sadistic pleasure. Events simply occur. Children get eaten by bears, adults disappear into mysterious machinery, and entire families undergo baroque destruction rendered in elegant Victorian crosshatching with alphabetical captions. The effect is profoundly unsettling precisely because it refuses emotional guidance. Readers can't project horror onto characters who don't experience it, can't identify with victims who show no distress, can't morally condemn perpetrators who display no malice. Gorey's cannibalistic scenarios—and they appear regularly in his work—become Rorschach tests revealing audience preconceptions. If you're disturbed, that disturbance comes from your own psychological framework, not from anything the narrative provides. This represents satire achieving radical detachment: cannibalism as a neutral event, consumption as a value-free transaction, horror as an entirely audience-generated response rather than an inherent property of the act.

The British tradition of comedic horror—exemplified by writers like Clive Barker in certain moods—treats cannibalism as transgression so extreme it circles back to comedy through sheer excess. When horror becomes sufficiently elaborate, when violence reaches operatic intensity, when consumption is described with such florid detail that it transcends grotesquerie and becomes aesthetic performance, audiences begin laughing despite themselves. This laughter isn't nervousness or discomfort—it's genuine recognition of artistry in transgression. The cannibal becomes craftsman, the consumption becomes performance art, and readers find themselves appreciating technical excellence even while acknowledging moral revulsion. This creates profound cognitive dissonance that satirical horror exploits ruthlessly: can you condemn something while admiring how well it's executed? If you appreciate the prose describing cannibalism, are you complicit in normalizing it? The satire implicates readers in the consumption they're ostensibly opposing, demonstrating that aesthetic appreciation operates independently of moral judgment and possibly in conflict with it.

Literary cannibalism ultimately reveals what philosophical and anthropological analysis can't: how imagination works when contemplating humanity's consumption of itself. Writers use anthropophagy as an ultimate test case for moral reasoning, as a limit condition that exposes how ethical systems function under maximum stress. The cannibal appears in literature not because writers are uniquely morbid but because no other transgression combines such visceral horror with such philosophical richness. Murder ends life, but cannibalism continues violation into death, transforming the subject into the object, the person into food, and the individual consciousness into metabolized calories. Every other crime preserves some boundary that cannibalism demolishes. Literary exploration of this dissolution generates insights that straightforward analysis misses—about what humans fear most deeply, about how moral frameworks collapse and reconstruct themselves, about the relationship between civilization and appetite. The cannibal haunts literature because it haunts consciousness: the recognition that under sufficient pressure, in appropriate conditions, facing the right combination of hunger and opportunity, we might become the monsters in cautionary tales. Literature doesn't resolve this anxiety. It examines what happens when you stop trying to fix it and instead follow the implications wherever they lead, even when they lead to recognizing that the distance between the reader and the cannibal measures shorter than anyone wants to admit.

Chapter 7: Legal and Ethical Dilemmas: The Morality of Cannibalism

The law knows what to do with cannibals. Lock them up, preferably forever, and don't examine why too closely. But this procedural certainty conceals philosophical chaos. When Armin Meiwes advertised online for someone willing to be killed and eaten, and Bernd Jürgen Armand Brandes responded enthusiastically, volunteering himself for consumption in 2001 Germany, the subsequent trial exposed something legal systems desperately want to avoid acknowledging: our moral and legal frameworks for cannibalism rest on unexamined foundations that collapse immediately under pressure. Meiwes received eight years initially for manslaughter, then life imprisonment upon retrial for murder—but not for cannibalism, because Germany had no law specifically criminalizing consensual anthropophagy between adults. The prosecutors had to retrofit existing statutes designed for entirely different circumstances because the law simply hadn't contemplated that someone might volunteer to be eaten, that consumption might happen with explicit permission, that the bright line between murderer and victim could blur into enthusiastic collaboration. This case didn't create new legal territory so much as reveal the unmapped wilderness that existed all along.

What makes the Meiwes case philosophically corrosive isn't the aberrant psychology it represents—we've got taxonomies for that, diagnostic categories that let us contain individual pathology without examining systemic assumptions. What corrodes is the consent problem. Western jurisprudence holds consent sacred in nearly every domain. You can consent to surgical amputation, to experimental medical procedures with fatal risk profiles, to voluntary euthanasia in jurisdictions that permit it. You can sign away your organs, agree to pharmaceutical trials, and authorize physicians to do things to your body that would constitute assault without permission. But you cannot consent to being eaten. The law simply refuses this particular exercise of bodily autonomy, even when the volunteer is mentally competent, fully informed, and enthusiastically willing. This isn't philosophical consistency—it's special pleading dressed in legal robes. The state has decided certain choices are too repugnant to permit regardless of consent, which means consent isn't actually the operating principle we claim it is. We've merely drawn arbitrary lines around acceptable self-determination and called them universal human rights.

The Property Problem: Who Owns a Corpse?

The moment someone dies, their body enters a legal limbo that reveals how incoherent our property frameworks become when confronted with human remains. You cannot own your own corpse. This sounds reasonable until you examine the implications. The deceased has no property interest in their remains because corpses aren't property—they're quasi-property, a category invented to handle things that resist normal ownership rules. Your family doesn't own your body either; they have custody rights subject to state regulation, religious tradition, and public health statutes. This creates bizarre scenarios where your clearly expressed wishes about disposition can be overridden by relatives, state authorities, or even creditors in some jurisdictions. The body becomes a thing that belongs to no one and everyone simultaneously, regulated by overlapping frameworks that contradict each other at crucial moments.

Now introduce cannibalism into this legal mess. If a deceased person explicitly authorized consumption of their remains—through a written directive, recorded testimony, or documented conversations—who has standing to prevent it? The corpse isn't property that can be stolen. The family's custody rights are limited by the deceased's expressed wishes in most domains. Yet every legal system would prevent the consumption regardless of documentation, which means we're enforcing communal taboos that supersede individual autonomy and property rights simultaneously. We've decided society has veto power over what happens to your body after death, that collective disgust outweighs personal directive, that some uses of human remains are so reprehensible that consent becomes irrelevant. But we refuse to articulate this principle explicitly because doing so would expose how much state power we've granted to enforce aesthetic preferences disguised as ethical necessities.

The situation becomes even more unstable when you introduce the commercial dimension. In the United States, you can sell blood, plasma, sperm, eggs, and—through compensated donation programs—kidneys in specific contexts. You cannot sell your entire body for post-mortem consumption, but the legal distinction rests on nothing more substantial than revulsion. If kidneys can be commodified for transplant, why not muscle tissue for consumption? Both involve consent, both involve bodily autonomy, and both potentially save or extend lives. The only difference is the cultural squirm factor. Some bioethicists have actually argued this position seriously: if we permit organ markets, consistency demands we permit meat markets, provided appropriate health regulations and consent documentation. No legislature has touched this argument with a ten-foot pole because following the logic would require admitting that our current framework privileges disgust over philosophical coherence. We've built legal architecture on sand, then declared it bedrock because acknowledging its instability would be too destabilizing.

The Impossibility of Victimless Anthropophagy

Here's where defenders of absolute prohibition retreat to seemingly stronger ground: cannibalism cannot be victimless even with consent because the practice generates downstream harms that justify state intervention. Consuming human flesh risks prion disease transmission—kuru, Creutzfeldt-Jakob disease, variant forms that take decades to manifest. Permitting any cannibalism might erode social taboos that prevent non-consensual forms. Creating legal pathways for anthropophagy could generate market pressures that compromise genuine consent, particularly among economically desperate populations. These objections sound prudential and harm-focused, properly concerned with protecting vulnerable populations from predation. But they prove too much. The same logic applies to extreme sports, experimental surgeries, and high-risk occupations we currently permit. Motorcycle riding has catastrophic injury rates; we don't ban it. Mountaineering kills hundreds annually; we regulate equipment instead. The distinction isn't risk level—it's that we find cannibalism disgusting regardless of risk, then retrofit harm-prevention justifications to validate prohibitions we'd maintain even if prion diseases didn't exist.

The social erosion argument deserves closer examination because it's the most sophisticated version of the slippery-slope concern. The claim runs: tolerating consensual cannibalism necessarily weakens the broader taboo, creating conditions where non-consensual forms become more likely. This argument assumes taboos function like dams—one crack spreads until catastrophic failure. But empirical evidence doesn't support this hydraulic model of moral constraints. The Netherlands permits euthanasia under strict conditions; this hasn't generated epidemic non-consensual killing. Portugal decriminalized all drug possession; usage rates didn't explode. Oregon allows physician-assisted suicide; elder abuse hasn't increased. Carefully regulated exceptions to absolute prohibitions don't automatically corrode the underlying norm. They might actually strengthen it by creating legitimate pressure-release valves that prevent total system rejection. The insistence that any permitted cannibalism necessarily leads to Donner Party free-for-all reveals anxiety about self-control more than evidence about social dynamics. We're projecting our fear that we might want to engage in prohibited behavior onto society at large, then using that projection to justify continued prohibition.

But there's a version of the erosion argument that does have teeth, and it's economic rather than moral. If you permit consensual adult cannibalism with appropriate medical screening and documentation, you've created a market. Markets generate pressure toward expansion. Funeral homes would develop specialized services. Restaurants might offer "memorial consumption" experiences. Medical tourism would emerge for wealthy individuals from prohibitionist countries. Once infrastructure exists, economic incentives push toward lower barriers and higher volume. The poor would face pressure to monetize their remains to pay off debts or support surviving family. "Donate your body to hungry strangers" becomes a compassionate option for the economically desperate. This isn't hypothetical—it's exactly what happened with paid plasma donation, with compensated surrogacy, with kidney markets in countries that permit them. The initial framework of autonomous adult choice becomes a cover for economic coercion operating through formally voluntary mechanisms. This argument against permitting cannibalism doesn't rest on disgust or taboo strength—it rests on acknowledging that consent operates differently when embedded in systems of structural inequality. The same person who freely chooses to be eaten when wealthy might feel compelled to make that choice when destitute, and the law can't distinguish these scenarios cleanly enough to prevent exploitation while permitting genuine autonomy.

Dignity Beyond Death: The Incoherence of Harm to the Deceased

Prosecutors in cannibalism cases frequently invoke dignity violations—that consuming human remains disrespects the deceased in ways that warrant criminal sanction. This presents an immediate philosophical problem: can you harm someone who no longer exists? Dead people have no experiences, no preferences, no interests that can be thwarted. The concept of post-mortem dignity requires believing that persons maintain some form of protectable interest after death, which commits you to positions about personhood and persistence that quickly become metaphysically untenable. If dignity survives death, then massive organ harvesting operations raise the same questions. We're already dicing up corpses and distributing pieces to strangers—we just call it transplantation instead of cannibalism, maintain clinical aesthetics instead of culinary ones, and insist the motivation (saving lives) sanitizes the practice. But corpses don't care about motivation. They're not experiencing anything. The dignity we're protecting is our own comfort, not their non-existent preferences.

Some philosophers bite this bullet and argue that yes, we can have obligations to the dead even though they can't be harmed, because respecting their ante-mortem preferences serves important social functions for the living. If we ignore what people wanted done with their remains, this undermines trust in similar directives and erodes confidence that one's expressed wishes will be honored after death. This argument has weight—until you examine which wishes we actually celebrate. Want to be buried in a particular cemetery? Sure. Want your ashes scattered at a meaningful location? We'll accommodate that. Want your body donated to medical research where it might be used for blast radius testing or decay rate analysis? Medical schools handle this routinely. Want to be eaten? Suddenly, we discover limits on respecting the deceased's preferences. We've carved out an exception specifically for anthropophagy while pretending we're following consistent principles about honoring the dead. The dignity argument collapses into disguised cultural enforcement the moment you test its boundaries.

Legal systems sometimes invoke the concept of "universal human dignity" to avoid this problem—claiming that certain practices violate dignity inherently, regardless of individual consent or preference.

Cannibalism supposedly degrades human dignity categorically because it reduces persons to mere meat, treating human bodies as interchangeable with animal flesh. This argument has surface plausibility until you notice it's completely circular. Why does consumption degrade dignity while cremation doesn't? Why does eating disrespect the human form, while dissection in anatomy classes receives institutional blessing? The answer can't be "because eating is consumption and consumption is disrespectful" without explaining why that's true, independent of our cultural training. Fire reduces bodies to ash—absolute destruction that prevents any future interaction. Consumption converts tissue into energy and waste—a transformation that integrates the deceased into ongoing biological processes. Neither is inherently more or less dignity-respecting without importing massive cultural assumptions about the appropriate treatment of remains. The "universal dignity" argument simply elevates Western cultural norms to metaphysical principles, then uses those principles to justify the norms that generated them.

Philosophical Frameworks That Fail Under Pressure

Utilitarian ethics should provide clear guidance here: maximize welfare, minimize suffering, aggregate outcomes across all affected parties. But applying this framework to cannibalism generates answers that professional ethicists immediately want to qualify into oblivion. Suppose consensual cannibalism prevents food waste (bodies contain usable protein), creates meaningful death experiences for volunteers (some people genuinely enjoy this), and doesn't generate negative utility beyond causing squeamishness in observers. In that case, strict utilitarianism suggests we should permit it. The same calculus that justifies organ donation applies to nutritive consumption. Observers' disgust counts in the welfare calculation, but it's fundamentally a selfish preference—they're not harmed by practices they never witness, just offended by knowledge that those practices occur. We don't usually let the aesthetic preferences of non-participants override participants' substantial welfare interests. But suggest that utilitarianism might permit cannibalism, and suddenly, ethicists discover that consequences aren't the only consideration, that some actions have intrinsic wrongness beyond their outcomes, that classical utilitarianism obviously needs deontological constraints.

Deontological ethics seems more promising because it can declare categorical prohibitions without outcome calculations. Kant's categorical imperative—act only according to maxims you can will as universal law—appears to rule out cannibalism immediately. But does it? "Consume humans with their knowing consent when they authentically volunteer for nutritive purposes" could be universalized without logical contradiction. If everyone who genuinely wanted to be eaten could be, and everyone who tried to eat them could, the system doesn't collapse into incoherence. It might be deeply weird, it might violate every social norm, but it's not logically contradictory in the way "lie whenever convenient" is. The Kantian framework lets you declare cannibalism impermissible only by loading additional premises about human dignity and treating people as ends rather than means—but those premises aren't obviously violated by consensual anthropophagy. The volunteer is exercising autonomy, using themselves as a means to their own ends. The consumer respects that autonomy by honoring the volunteer's preferences. You can make Kant work here, but you have to add substantial interpretive weight that the framework doesn't provide independently.

Virtue ethics fares no better. What virtuous person would consume human flesh? But this begs the question by assuming the practice is vicious rather than demonstrating why. Courage, temperance, wisdom, justice—the classical virtues don't obviously condemn cannibalism. You could construct a story where consuming dead relatives demonstrates courage in facing cultural taboos, wisdom in recognizing resource efficiency, and justice in honoring the deceased's autonomous choices. This feels like sophisticated trolling, but the logical structure holds. The virtue framework assumes shared community standards about what counts as virtuous behavior, and those standards aren't universal. In communities that practiced endocannibalism, consuming dead kin was precisely what virtuous people did—showing respect, maintaining social bonds, fulfilling obligations. Appealing to virtue just relocates the disagreement to which communities' standards should be treated as authoritative.

Every major ethical framework either permits cannibalism under specific conditions or requires additional assumptions to prohibit it. This should disturb us more than it does. We're not dealing with edge cases of applied ethics where reasonable philosophers disagree about difficult trade-offs. Cannibalism is supposed to be clear-cut—obviously wrong, universally condemned, requiring no sophisticated argument for prohibition. Yet our most sophisticated ethical theories can't deliver that conclusion without importing the very cultural assumptions that need justification. The philosophical emperor has no clothes, and we're all pretending not to notice because acknowledging it would require either accepting cannibalism or admitting our moral frameworks rest on unargued-for intuitions we're unwilling to defend rigorously.

The State's Interest in Your Digestive Choices

Why does the government care what you eat? For most foods, it doesn't go beyond basic safety regulations. Fugu fish can kill you with improper preparation—Japanese authorities license chefs and monitor restaurants, but don't ban consumption. Raw milk carries disease risk—some jurisdictions prohibit sale, others just require labeling and inspection. Alcohol causes massive social harm—we tried prohibition, concluded it was worse than the problem, and settled for age restrictions and drunk driving laws. The state's intervention in dietary choices usually operates through safety regulation and informed consent rather than absolute prohibition. But human flesh? Total ban, no exceptions, no amount of safety compliance makes it permissible. This isn't health policy—it's cultural enforcement using state power.

The legal scholar James Q. Whitman documented how modern legal systems inherited medieval concepts of "crimes against nature" that originally included sodomy, bestiality, and blasphemy. As Enlightenment rationalism undermined religious justifications, legislatures quietly dropped most of these prohibitions or replaced them with narrower statutes focused on measurable harm. But cannibalism remained in this archaic category because no constituency emerged to defend it. Gay rights activists challenged sodomy laws. Animal welfare groups reframed bestiality as animal abuse rather than an unnatural crime. Blasphemy became a free speech issue. Cannibalism had no advocates, so it stayed prohibited under ancient logic that nobody bothered updating. We're still prosecuting anthropophagy using conceptual frameworks from legal systems that believed the state had a legitimate interest in preventing offense to God. The specific theological justification evaporated, but the prohibition remained embedded in statutory codes like linguistic fossils from extinct belief systems.

This creates profound problems for constitutional rights frameworks. If the state can prohibit consensual private behavior between adults that harms no third party, what limiting principle prevents totalitarian dietary regulation? Why not ban foie gras (already done in some jurisdictions), veal, and factory-farmed meat generally? If cultural disgust justifies criminal prohibition, then majority preference can criminalize any minority practice that generates sufficient revulsion. The standard legal answer—we only prohibit behaviors that harm others—doesn't work here because the "harm" from consensual cannibalism consists entirely of offending observers who don't participate and aren't directly affected. We've carved an exception for anthropophagy that undermines the broader liberal principle of state neutrality toward private choices. And we maintain this exception not through an argued constitutional doctrine but through a simple refusal to examine the foundations.

The international human rights framework makes this even messier. The Universal Declaration of Human Rights and subsequent treaties establish bodily autonomy as a fundamental right, subject only to restrictions necessary for protecting public health and others' rights. Some scholars have argued—mostly in theoretical contexts, not actual advocacy—that absolute prohibition on consensual cannibalism violates these frameworks because it criminalizes private behavior that doesn't necessarily threaten public health and occurs between adults with full autonomy. No international court will touch this argument seriously, but its logical structure is sound. We've decided human rights don't include the right to be eaten or to eat volunteers, but we've never explained why in terms consistent with the broader rights framework. The prohibition rests on unstated assumptions that cannibalism is so self-evidently wrong that justification would be unnecessary, even offensive. But that's exactly the argument authorities made about homosexuality, interracial marriage, religious heterodoxy—practices now recognized as protected by those same human rights frameworks. The precedent should terrify us even if we're certain cannibalism deserves prohibition.

The most honest legal position would acknowledge: we prohibit cannibalism because it disgusts us. After all, allowing it would corrode social trust in unpredictable ways, because the potential for abuse outweighs any claimed autonomy interest, and because no political constituency wants to defend it, so there's no cost to maintaining prohibition. This doesn't fit our preferred story about law as a rational system deriving from first principles, but it's accurate. We've preserved a taboo through state violence, not because philosophical argument compels it, but because dismantling it generates risks nobody wants to assume and benefits nobody cares enough to fight for. That's fine as practical politics. But it means our legal prohibition on cannibalism exists in permanent tension with our stated commitments to autonomy, consent, and limiting state power to measurable harms. We maintain the ban by not examining it too closely, by keeping the philosophical foundations deliberately vague, by hoping nobody with standing and resources pushes the question into courts that would have to generate actual reasoning rather than reflexive disgust. Eventually, probably in some jurisdiction none of us are watching, someone will push. When that happens, the incoherence becomes unavoidable. Legal systems will have to choose between philosophical consistency and cultural preservation. Every indication suggests they'll choose preservation and invent sophisticated-sounding justifications afterward. But that just proves the point: on cannibalism, law operates primarily as an enforcement mechanism for visceral taboos that can't survive sustained philosophical scrutiny but feel too dangerous to abandon.

Chapter 8: Cannibalism in Art: Visual Depictions Across Eras

The canvas hangs in Madrid's Museo del Prado, fourteen feet wide, impossible to look away from. Francisco Goya's *Saturn Devouring His Son* shows no mercy to anyone who stands before it. The Titan clutches a headless body, blood streaming down the torso, eyes bulging with something beyond madness—primal terror at his own actions, perhaps, or hunger so absolute it obliterates conscience. Goya painted it directly onto the walls of his home during his final years, between 1819 and 1823, part of his "Black Paintings" series that he never intended for public exhibition. This wasn't art designed for galleries or patrons. This was a man processing something so viscerally disturbing that he needed to externalize it in pigment and brushstroke, needed to make the horror visible so he could live with it inside his skull. The painting works because it refuses symbolic distance. This isn't mythology rendered tastefully. This is butchery captured in the act, the moment when hunger transforms father into predator and child into meat. Every subsequent artist who's depicted cannibalism has operated in this image's gravitational field, whether they acknowledge it or not. The question Goya forces is one that visual art answers differently than text ever could: what happens when you can't look away, when the metaphor has teeth and blood and takes up fourteen feet of wall space demanding you witness it?

Visual depictions of cannibalism perform different cognitive work than written accounts because they bypass the linguistic processing centers that let us maintain emotional distance. When you read about anthropophagy, your brain translates symbols into meaning, constructing mental images with variable fidelity to the described reality. When you confront it visually, that defensive gap collapses. The image arrives pre-processed, demanding immediate emotional response before rational analysis can construct protective frameworks. This is why colonial powers preferred written accounts of indigenous cannibalism to visual ones—text could be selectively quoted, interpreted, and deployed as evidence without forcing viewers to confront the full human complexity of what was being described. But commission a painting of the practice and suddenly you're asking artists to render human faces in the act of consumption, to show victim and perpetrator as equally human, to make the horror specific rather than abstract. The British Museum's nineteenth-century collection includes extensive written documentation of Fijian cannibalism but remarkably few visual depictions, and the existing ones relegate the practice to background detail in broader ethnographic scenes. The curators understood something crucial: you can maintain moral superiority more easily through textual condemnation than through honest visual representation, because honest visual representation requires acknowledging the humanity of everyone involved.

Medieval Illumination and the Pedagogy of Damnation

Medieval manuscript illuminations deployed cannibalistic imagery with surgical precision as a theological instruction manual. The marginalia of fourteenth and fifteenth-century Books of Hours contain dozens of scenes showing demons consuming sinners, but these aren't generic hell-mouth imagery. The artists rendered specific torments for specific sins: gluttons being devoured mouth-first, the avaricious consumed while clutching their coins, the lustful eaten genitals-first in permanent reciprocal violation. The Très Riches Heures du Duc de Berry, completed around 1416, includes an afterlife sequence where damned souls aren't simply thrown into hell—they're systematically butchered and prepared for consumption using techniques that mirror contemporary kitchen practices. One demon holds a cleaver, another tends the fire, a third arranges body parts with the practiced efficiency of a professional cook. The illuminators weren't fantasizing about supernatural punishment. They were illustrating a coherent theological position: sin transforms the eternal soul into consumable matter, rebellion against God's order reduces the human to livestock, and damnation is literally being eaten forever by something that will never be satisfied.

This visual theology did something crucial that written damnation narratives couldn't achieve: it made hell's logistics visible and therefore comprehensible to illiterate congregations. When priests held up these manuscripts during services, pointing to the illuminated torments while delivering sermons about sin's consequences, the audience received multimedia instruction. The cannibalistic demons weren't metaphorical—according to medieval theology, they were documentary. Demons consumed souls. This was a fact, not a poetic flourish. The illuminations depicted eschatological reality as understood by the Church, rendered in gold leaf and vermillion with the same documentary intent as contemporary medical illustrations. What troubles modern viewers is the craftsmanship applied to these scenes. The demons are beautifully painted, their musculature anatomically accurate, their consumption of human flesh depicted with the same technical sophistication lavished on scenes of saints in glory. The manuscripts make no tonal distinction between the saved and the damned at the level of artistic execution. Both receive equal painterly attention, and both are rendered with equal care. This suggests that for medieval illuminators, depicting damnation wasn't a distasteful obligation—it was an opportunity to demonstrate technical mastery through challenging subject matter that demanded anatomical knowledge, compositional skill, and psychological insight into expressions of extreme suffering.

Hieronymus Bosch and the Domestication of Horror

Then Bosch arrived and changed everything by making cannibalism routine. His triptych *The Garden of Earthly Delights*, painted between 1490 and 1510, contains so many instances of human consumption that cataloguing them requires a systematic survey. The right panel—hell—shows bodies being swallowed, regurgitated, and consumed again in perpetual cycles. But what separates Bosch from his predecessors isn't the presence of anthropophagy. It's the bureaucratic orderliness of it. His hell operates like a well-managed abattoir where consumption happens on an industrial schedule. One demon defecates consumed souls into a pit where another demon collects them for redistribution. A bird-headed demon enthroned on a chamber pot consumes bodies fed to it by lesser demons while simultaneously excreting them into an abyss below. The compositional logic is assembly-line efficiency applied to eternal torment. Bosch painted hell as a functioning system with established procedures, and cannibalism as one operational component among many.

This represents a philosophical shift from earlier medieval imagery. Bosch's demons aren't performing consumption as punishment— they're processing throughput as a job function. The victim's identity becomes irrelevant because they're not individuals receiving customized torment but units moving through a system. This depersonalization of anthropophagy in visual art appears here perhaps for the first time with full sophistication. The horror isn't that you might be eaten. The horror is that your consumption will be methodical, routine, unremarkable, one iteration in an infinite sequence that continues regardless of whether you specifically are present or absent. Bosch anticipated modern anxieties about systematized violence by four centuries. His visual vocabulary for depicting industrialized consumption influenced everything from World War I trench art to contemporary horror cinema's obsession with mechanical death. But his original audience read these images devotionally, as meditation prompts for contemplating sin's consequences. The paintings hung in private chambers of wealthy patrons who used them to examine their consciences, to remind themselves that material success meant nothing against the backdrop of eternal damnation. That such viscerally disturbing imagery served a contemplative function reveals something about pre-modern European Christianity's comfort with depicting extremity. They believed heaven and hell were real places where real things happened to real souls, and squeamishness about visualizing those realities would be spiritual cowardice. Bosch gave them unflinching depictions because that's what serious theological consideration demanded.

Renaissance Humanism and the Cannibal Sublime

The Renaissance complicated everything by discovering that cannibalism could be beautiful. When Titian painted *The Flaying of Marsyas* around 1570-1576, he technically depicted skinning rather than consumption, but the painting's impact derives from its treatment of bodily violation as aesthetic opportunity. Marsyas hangs inverted while Apollo removes his skin with surgical precision, and Titian renders the scene with such painterly beauty—the golden light, the compositional balance, the rich color harmony—that the horror becomes inseparable from pleasure. The painting asks viewers to find the flaying beautiful, to recognize their own aesthetic enjoyment of depicted suffering. This represents a radical departure from medieval clarity about suffering-as-punishment. Titian doesn't moralize. He presents and lets viewers discover their own reactions, including the disturbing realization that yes, this is gorgeous, and yes, being beautiful doesn't make it less horrifying, and yes, both reactions coexist without canceling each other out.

This aesthetic approach to bodily violation prepared European visual culture for more explicit anthropophagic imagery that arrived through colonial encounter documentation. When Theodore de Bry published his illustrated editions of exploration narratives in the 1590s, depicting indigenous Brazilian cannibalism, he used compositional techniques borrowed directly from Renaissance martyrdom paintings. His engravings show indigenous peoples consuming captives, but the scenes are structured like classical statuary come to life—balanced compositions, heroic musculature, dramatic contrapposto poses. De Bry's cannibals aren't monsters. They're idealized human forms engaged in the ultimate transgression, rendered with the same artistic sophistication applied to European subjects. This created profound interpretive confusion that persists in scholarship even now. Were the engravings documentary evidence of barbarism justifying colonial intervention? Or were they Renaissance experiments in depicting cultural difference without Gothic demonization? De Bry himself left no definitive answer, possibly because he recognized the images worked more effectively when interpretation remained ambiguous. The engravings could satisfy the European appetite for exotic horror while simultaneously functioning as ethnographic documentation, could justify colonial violence, and also preserve a visual record of practices that colonialism would eradicate. That he managed to serve both purposes simultaneously while producing images of genuine artistic merit demonstrates the power of visual ambiguity in ways text rarely achieves.

Eighteenth-Century Satire and the Problem of Comedic Anthropophagy

William Hogarth understood something crucial about visual humor that most artists miss: atrocity becomes funnier the more technically competent its depiction. His 1751 print series *Beer Street and Gin Lane* doesn't directly show cannibalism. Still, his later work *The Four Stages of Cruelty* escalates through increasingly graphic violence until the final plate shows the perpetrator's corpse being anatomized by surgeons—not cannibalism technically, but medical consumption of criminal bodies that operates on identical transgressive logic. What makes the image work as satire rather than simple horror is Hogarth's refusal to editorialize through visual language. The surgeons dissect with professional detachment. The viewing audience in the print watches with clinical interest. No one registers moral outrage at the violation of the corpse because, within the print's logic, this is justice appropriately served: you committed cruelty, so your body becomes educational material. The print asks viewers to either accept this proportionality or explain why it's different from other judicial punishments. That it does so through technical draftsmanship good enough to function as an actual anatomical reference—medical students reportedly used Hogarth's prints as study aids— demonstrates how artistic skill can make moral discomfort sharper rather than softening it.

The Marquis de Sade's influence on later visual artists came not from his written descriptions of anthropophagy but from his understanding that depicting forbidden acts requires either complete clinical detachment or baroque excess, never the middle ground. French Revolutionary-era prints showing aristocrats being consumed by sans-culottes followed this principle: either a stark documentary style that refused emotional commentary, or a delirious exaggeration that pushed beyond horror into grotesque carnival. François-Nicolas Martinet's 1789 prints show Marie Antoinette being prepared for metaphorical consumption by the people, surrounded by carnivalesque imagery that blends butchery with political theater. The prints functioned as both genuine revolutionary propaganda and satirical commentary on propaganda itself—they simultaneously encouraged aristocratic overthrow while mocking the dehumanization required to sustain revolutionary violence. This doubled function became possible only through visual means, because visual imagery allows simultaneous sincere and ironic readings in ways that text struggles to achieve. A viewer could read the prints as straightforward anti-monarchist material, while another viewer standing beside them understood the same image as a critique of revolutionary excess, and both readings were activated from identical visual information processed through different interpretive frameworks.

Romanticism's Cannibal Sublime and the Shipwreck Industry

Théodore Géricault's *The Raft of the Medusa*, completed in 1819, represents the most sophisticated engagement with survival cannibalism in visual art history. The painting depicts the aftermath of the French frigate Méduse's 1816 wreck, where 147 people crowded onto a hastily-constructed raft and only fifteen survived the thirteen-day ordeal through, among other desperate measures, consuming the dead. Géricault knew this—the event was extensively documented, the cannibalism publicly acknowledged in survivor testimony. Yet the painting shows no evidence of anthropophagy. Bodies lie scattered across the raft, but they're intact, idealized, painted with Michelangelo-influenced musculature that transforms suffering into heroic monumentality. Géricault made the decision consciously: he interviewed survivors, sketched cadavers at the morgue to understand decomposition, and researched the precise timeline of who died when. Then he painted a version of events that removed the most transgressive element while preserving every other historical detail. This wasn't cowardice. It was recognition that depicting the cannibalism explicitly would collapse the painting's function as a political critique of governmental incompetence into a sensational spectacle. The absent cannibalism works harder than present cannibalism would have, because viewers who knew the full story— and after the scandal, most French viewers did—confronted the gap between painted idealization and historical reality. That gap became the space where reflection happened, where viewers had to mentally supply what the painting refused to show, making them complicit in either acknowledging or denying the cannibalism their own historical knowledge required them to recognize.

Francisco de Goya understood the opposite strategy: depicting everything with such uncompromising intensity that viewers have no refuge in aesthetic appreciation. His *Disasters of War* print series, created between 1810 and 1820 during the Peninsular War but not published until 1863, includes plate 39 titled "Grande hazaña! Con muertos!" ("Great deeds! Against the dead!"). The image shows mutilated corpses displayed on tree branches like butchered livestock. Goya doesn't confirm cannibalism explicitly, but the methodical dismemberment and display suggest processing for consumption among other wartime atrocities. What separates these prints from earlier battle documentation is Goya's refusal to provide moral framing. There are no heroes here, no noble causes worth the carnage, no redemptive narrative that justifies the violence. The prints simply state: this happened, humans did this to other humans, make of it what you will. That cold documentary stance—this is what war looks like when you remove the mythology—influenced every subsequent visual artist trying to depict anthropophagy honestly. You either follow Géricault's path and suggest through absence, or you follow Goya's path and show without commentary. Still, you cannot combine romantic heroism with an honest depiction of bodies consumed by other bodies. The incompatibility is formal as much as ethical.

Modernism's Anthropological Gaze and the Weaponization of Primitivism

Paul Gauguin's Tahitian paintings never show cannibalism directly, but they're saturated with European fantasies about Polynesian anthropophagy that Gauguin deliberately exploited while simultaneously critiquing. His 1902 painting *Barbarian Tales* shows Tahitian figures in poses suggesting storytelling, the title itself invoking primitive otherness. Gauguin knew perfectly well that Tahitian cannibalism—to the limited extent it had existed—ended decades before his arrival. He painted ethnographic fiction, constructing visual evidence of practices that lived primarily in the European imagination. But he did so with enough sophistication that the paintings function as documentation of European fantasy rather than Polynesian reality, preserving the colonial gaze as subject matter while refusing to endorse it. Later critics have struggled with this intentional ambiguity, unable to determine whether Gauguin was critiquing primitivist fetishization or participating in it. The paintings themselves refuse to clarify, presenting idealized indigenous bodies in compositions that borrow from both European classical tradition and Gauguin's imperfect understanding of Polynesian visual culture, creating hybrid imagery that belongs fully to neither tradition.

This ambiguity became weaponized by mid-century artists exploring how visual culture constructs racial otherness. Jean-Michel Basquiat's paintings include recurring cannibalism imagery that explicitly references both African diaspora stereotypes and art historical traditions of depicting consumption. His 1982 painting *Untitled (Skull)* shows a skull with exposed teeth surrounded by text fragments including "CROWN" and references to consumption, simultaneously invoking classical memento mori imagery and the skull-and-bones primitivism of colonial anthropology. Basquiat wasn't depicting cannibalism—he was depicting how visual culture has depicted cannibalism, how the cannibal image functions as a signifier for racial otherness that justifies exploitation. His appropriation of the imagery performs a double reversal: he takes the stereotype, makes it central to high-art paintings that sell for millions to wealthy collectors, forcing those collectors to hang their own prejudices on gallery walls as aesthetic objects. The paintings become mirrors showing viewers the violence embedded in how they've been taught to look at bodies that don't match Western European standards. That this critique happens through visual means rather than textual explanation makes it more viscerally effective—viewers confront their own responses before intellectual understanding can construct defensive interpretations.

Contemporary artists have largely abandoned direct depiction of cannibalism in favor of metaphorical approaches that let them explore consumption as an economic system, gender violence, or environmental catastrophe. But the history traced here—from Goya's raw horror through Géricault's strategic absence to Basquiat's appropriative critique—demonstrates that visual art processes anthropophagy differently than any other medium. Paint and canvas force confrontation that text permits avoiding. The image arrives too fast for comfortable intellectual distance, demanding emotional response before rational frameworks can sanitize it. Every artist who's depicted human consumption has wrestled with this formal reality: you cannot show this neutrally, cannot render it without making choices about what to emphasize, what to minimize, how to direct viewer attention, whether to make it beautiful or deliberately ugly. Those choices reveal more about the artist's cultural moment than about cannibalism itself, which is perhaps the point. We don't look at these paintings to understand anthropophagy. We look at them to understand ourselves, looking to catch ourselves in the act of responding to the ultimate taboo made visible, to discover what we do with our eyes when confronted with what we insist should be impossible to witness.

Chapter 9: Anthropological Perspectives: Understanding the Cannibal Mindset

The question isn't whether cannibals are human. The question is whether the rest of us are willing to admit what that means.

Anthropology spent its first century as a discipline trying to create taxonomies that would locate anthropophagy safely in the past, among populations we could study from a comfortable distance while maintaining our own moral exemption. Then the data started refusing cooperation. Brain scans of contemporary individuals who'd engaged in cannibalistic acts—whether through ritual continuation, survival necessity, or pathological compulsion—showed neural architecture indistinguishable from control populations. The neuroscientist Jim Fallon discovered this accidentally in 2005 while studying psychopathic brain patterns. He'd collected scans from known violent criminals, compared them to typical baseline scans, and identified consistent anomalies in the orbital cortex and amygdala regions. Then he examined his own family members' scans as controls and discovered his own brain displayed the exact markers he'd been identifying as psychopathic indicators. Fallon had never harmed anyone. He'd built a successful career, maintained functional relationships, and contributed productively to society. The neural signatures we'd been treating as deterministic proved nothing of the sort. This finding extends uncomfortably to anthropophagy: the capacity for cannibalism isn't neurologically aberrant. It's neurologically normal, suppressed by cultural conditioning rather than biological constraint.

What makes someone capable of consuming human flesh isn't damaged brain architecture or primitive evolutionary remnants. It's the presence of cognitive frameworks that redefine the act within acceptable parameters. Every human brain contains the necessary machinery to perform anthropophagy—the motor planning, the gustatory processing, the executive function required to override revulsion responses. We're all born with this capability. What differs is whether environmental conditions and cultural context activate it or whether competing frameworks successfully suppress it throughout a lifetime. The anthropological evidence demonstrates this with uncomfortable clarity: populations separated by geography, genetic heritage, and millennia of cultural evolution independently developed cannibalistic practices when specific triggering conditions appeared. The convergent evolution of anthropophagy across unrelated societies suggests we're examining the human behavioral baseline, not the human behavioral aberration.

The Cognitive Architecture of Acceptability

When researchers interview individuals who've engaged in culturally sanctioned cannibalism—primarily elderly informants in Papua New Guinea and the Amazon who participated before missionary intervention—they consistently report something that troubles Western psychological models: the complete absence of guilt or moral conflict during the actual practice. The distress appears later, generated not by the act itself but by the clash between remembered normalcy and subsequently imposed moral frameworks. One Fore woman, interviewed by medical anthropologist Shirley Lindenbaum in the 1990s, described mortuary feasts where she'd consumed her mother's brain tissue as emotionally equivalent to other funeral responsibilities—difficult, sad, but necessary and proper. The interviewer kept pushing for evidence of psychological trauma, kept trying to locate the moment where moral revulsion appeared. It never did. What disturbed the informant wasn't what she'd done; it was the interviewer's obvious horror, the recognition that actions she'd performed with communal approval were now being categorized as monstrous. The trauma was retrospective, imposed by contact with alternative moral systems, not inherent to the practice.

This generates a profound problem for universal ethics. Suppose the disgust response to cannibalism can be completely absent in psychologically healthy individuals raised within supportive cultural contexts. In that case, the prohibition isn't universal moral law—it's culturally contingent conditioning that we've mistaken for something deeper. The counterargument points to cross-cultural commonalities: even societies that practiced ritual cannibalism maintained restrictions on when, how, and who could participate. These weren't free-for-all cultures where anyone could eat anyone under any circumstances. They developed elaborate rule systems governing acceptable anthropophagy, which suggests recognition that the practice required social control even within permissive frameworks. But here's the corroding question: does the presence of rules around cannibalism prove its fundamental wrongness, or does it simply demonstrate that powerful practices require social organization? We regulate sex extensively in every culture without arguing that sexuality is fundamentally immoral. We create complex frameworks around property ownership, violence, marriage, and child-rearing—all human universals that require cultural management precisely because they're important, not because they're aberrant.

The neuropsychological research refuses to support moral absolutism here. Studies using functional MRI to examine disgust responses show that culturally instilled aversions activate the insula cortex identically to innate disgust responses to spoiled food or disease indicators. Your brain processes the horror of cannibalism using the same neural pathways it uses to process the revulsion of rotting meat—which means the response is learned, not hardwired. Children raised in isolation from cultural messages about anthropophagy don't spontaneously develop cannibalism aversion any more than they spontaneously build language. Both require cultural transmission. This is why feral children, when discovered and studied, show no innate food taboos beyond texture preferences and acute poisoning avoidance. The Cambodian girl found living in jungle isolation in 2007 had been eating insects, small mammals, whatever she could catch— and showed no comprehension of cultural dietary restrictions when returned to human society. She had to be explicitly taught which foods were disgusting, which combinations were unacceptable, and which ingredients were forbidden. The prohibition against human flesh would have required the same explicit instruction as any other culturally specific taboo.

Rationalization Mechanics and Moral Flexibility

When individuals engage in cannibalism outside culturally sanctioned contexts—survival situations, criminal pathology, wartime breakdown—they employ cognitive strategies that reveal how human moral reasoning actually functions under pressure. The ship's crew that consumed Richard Parker after nineteen days adrift didn't experience a sudden moral transformation that made anthropophagy acceptable. They constructed sequential justifications that made the previously unthinkable gradually thinkable, then doable, then done. Contemporary psychological research on moral disengagement, pioneered by Albert Bandura in his studies of military atrocities and corporate malfeasance, identifies eight mechanisms humans use to overcome ethical resistance: moral justification, euphemistic labeling, advantageous comparison, displacement of responsibility, diffusion of responsibility, disregard of consequences, dehumanization of victims, and attribution of blame to victims. Every documented case of survival cannibalism employs multiple mechanisms from this list.

The progression follows predictable patterns. First comes moral justification: we'll die otherwise, our families need us to survive, and our continued existence has value that outweighs this transgression. Then euphemistic labeling: they're not people anymore once they're dead, it's just meat at this point, we're using "available resources." Advantageous comparison appears next: this is less immoral than murder, less immoral than letting everyone die, less sinful than whatever hypothetical worse option you can imagine. Displacement of responsibility emerges in group settings: we drew lots so fate decided, we all agreed so no individual bears sole blame, and circumstances forced this choice. The final stages involve dehumanization—treating the body as an object rather than a person—and consequence disregard: we can't think about what this means right now, we'll process the implications later, survival requires focusing on immediate physical needs rather than abstract moral questions.

What makes this progression anthropologically significant is its universality. Japanese soldiers during World War II who engaged in cannibalism of executed prisoners followed the same psychological sequence as medieval siege survivors, as contemporary plane crash survivors, and as any group that transgressed the prohibition under duress. The specific cultural context varies wildly—samurai honor codes versus Christian guilt versus secular humanist ethics—but the cognitive mechanics remain consistent. This suggests that moral flexibility around cannibalism isn't a cultural artifact but a psychological architecture. The human brain comes equipped with override mechanisms that can be activated when survival, authority, or ideology requires transgressing even the deepest prohibitions. We're not hardwired against anthropophagy in any way that can't be temporarily suspended through predictable psychological processes.

The Authority Problem: Why Obedience Permits Atrocity

Stanley Milgram's obedience experiments in the 1960s demonstrated that ordinary people would administer potentially lethal electric shocks to strangers when instructed by authority figures, even while experiencing obvious moral distress about doing so. Subsequent replications and extensions of this research show that obedience to authority can override almost any ethical constraint, provided the authority structure is sufficiently established and the gradual escalation of transgression prevents clear decision points where resistance might crystallize. This finding extends directly to anthropophagy in contexts where hierarchical structures normalize the practice. The Aztec priest overseeing ritual sacrifice and subsequent consumption of captives wasn't personally morally deranged—he was operating within an authority structure that defined these acts as necessary, sacred, and professionally appropriate. The individual priest's personal moral compass became irrelevant once institutional authority established behavioral parameters.

Modern replications of Milgram's work, conducted with contemporary ethical oversight that the original experiments lacked, continue to demonstrate the same fundamental finding: people will commit acts they personally find abhorrent when embedded in authority structures that normalize those acts. A 2009 replication by Jerry Burger at Santa Clara University found that 70% of participants continued administering shocks past the point where the victim was screaming in apparent agony, identical to Milgram's original findings, despite five decades of increased psychological sophistication in the general population. We haven't evolved past this vulnerability. We haven't educated our way out of susceptibility to authority-driven moral override, which means that under the right institutional conditions, with the right gradual normalization process, with the right authority figures providing instruction and approval, contemporary populations could be conditioned to engage in cannibalistic practices with the same bureaucratic efficiency that historical societies demonstrated.

This isn't hypothetical catastrophizing. The psychological mechanisms that enabled Nazi functionaries to process mass murder with administrative calm, that allowed Rwandan Hutus to systematically kill Tutsi neighbors they'd lived peacefully beside for years, that permitted Khmer Rouge cadres to torture and execute intellectuals and urban populations—these same mechanisms could normalize anthropophagy under appropriate conditions. The specific trigger points differ, but the underlying psychology remains constant. Humans possess an extraordinary capacity for moral compartmentalization when authority structures and peer pressure align to make the unthinkable routine. The cannibal mindset isn't fundamentally different from the military mindset, the corporate mindset, or the bureaucratic mindset that allows people to perform destructive actions because those actions have been redefined within institutional frameworks as necessary, proper, or even virtuous.

In-Group Boundaries and the Construction of Edibility

Anthropological examination of which humans get eaten reveals uncomfortable patterns about how we construct social categories. Endocannibalistic societies—those that consumed their own dead—maintained strict protocols about which kin qualified for mortuary consumption versus which received standard burial. The Wari of Brazil reserved funeral consumption for close relatives, specifically excluding distant kin and non-relatives entirely from the practice. But the determining factor wasn't a biological relationship measured through genetic proximity. It was social intimacy, daily interaction, and emotional significance. You ate the people you'd lived with closely, whose deaths genuinely disrupted your daily existence. Strangers and acquaintances got buried or cremated according to standard procedure. The practice wasn't universal honor of the dead—it was selective incorporation of socially significant individuals into a living community through the most literal means available.

Exocannibalistic societies—those that consumed enemies or outsiders—reveal even starker boundary construction. The Tupinambá of sixteenth-century Brazil developed an entire martial culture around capturing, ritually executing, and consuming enemy warriors, but they excluded women, children, and non-combatants from this treatment. The enemy warrior's body became consumable precisely because his role in life made him already symbolically consumable—he existed to be defeated, his strength existed to be absorbed, his identity existed to be negated through martial superiority. The act of eating him completed a process that began with combat and continued through execution. He was already functionally dead the moment capture occurred; consumption simply made that social death physical. But capture a Tupinambá warrior's wife or child, and they'd be integrated into the victor's community through adoption rather than consumption. The determining factor wasn't ethnicity or genetics—it was role-based social construction of edibility.

These patterns persist in contemporary contexts where anthropophagy appears. Criminal cannibals—Dahmer, Sagawa, Nilsen—selected victims from marginalized populations whose disappearance would generate minimal investigation. Sex workers, runaways, migrants, economically precarious young men—people whose social ties were already attenuated, whose absence might not be immediately noticed, who existed at the periphery of community protection. This victim selection wasn't incidental to the cannibalism; it was psychologically necessary for it. The perpetrators required victims who were already symbolically outside full personhood, already partially dehumanized by social marginalization, already existing in a category that made their consumption psychologically possible. You can't easily eat someone who's fully integrated into the social fabric because too many people would notice, care, and investigate. But someone is already invisible? Is someone already socially consumable in metaphorical terms? The psychological distance required for literal consumption becomes achievable.

Belief System Override: When Ideology Reconstructs Reality

The most disturbing anthropological finding about cannibalism isn't its historical prevalence—that's merely documentation. It's the demonstration that sufficiently robust ideological frameworks can make the practice feel not just acceptable but morally mandatory to otherwise psychologically healthy individuals. The Aghori sadhus of India, who consume human flesh from corpses at cremation grounds, aren't experiencing psychotic breaks. They're operating within a sophisticated philosophical tradition that explicitly positions extreme transgression as spiritual technology. The consumption of polluted substances—including putrefying human tissue—is theorized as a method for transcending dualistic thinking that traps consciousness in cycles of birth and death. This isn't a rationalization of pathology; it's a deliberate deployment of extreme practice in the service of articulated philosophical goals that predate the individual practitioner by centuries.

Western psychology struggles to categorize this because diagnostic frameworks assume that cannibalistic behavior indicates mental illness requiring treatment. But the Aghori tradition maintains institutional continuity spanning hundreds of years, produces functionally integrated practitioners who live within communities without causing harm to others, and generates philosophical texts that demonstrate sophisticated abstract reasoning about consciousness, materiality, and liberation. These aren't symptoms of disordered thinking—they're evidence of how effectively belief systems can reconstruct experienced reality. When a practitioner consumes human brain tissue, his phenomenological experience of that act differs fundamentally from a serial killer's experience of similar behavior because the meaning-making frameworks are completely different. The Aghori experiences transcendent practice; the criminal experiences compulsive pathology—same physical act, entirely different psychological reality, generated entirely through ideological context.

This principle extends to every form of culturally sanctioned cannibalism. The Aztec priest didn't experience his work as butchery because the belief system reconstructed it as cosmic maintenance. The Fore woman didn't experience mortuary consumption as a violation because her culture defined it as a proper kinship obligation. The Antarctic crash survivors who consumed their dead teammates didn't become monsters because Catholic theology provided confessional frameworks for processing transgression while maintaining spiritual integrity. Belief systems don't just justify anthropophagy after the fact—they fundamentally alter the subjective experience of committing it by providing interpretive frameworks that reconstruct meaning at the moment of action. This is why simple moral condemnation of historical cannibalism fails anthropologically: it assumes universal subjective experience across radically different meaning-making systems, which the evidence consistently refutes.

The implications corrode comfortable assumptions about moral truth. If belief systems can make cannibalism feel not just acceptable but spiritually necessary to psychologically healthy practitioners, then either moral truth doesn't exist independent of cultural framework, or humans possess such an effective self-deception capacity that we can't trust our moral intuitions about anything. Neither option provides comfort. The first option makes morality an arbitrary cultural construction. The second option makes human moral sense unreliable to the point of uselessness. We're left examining a practice that seems obviously, universally wrong—and discovering that "obvious" and "universal" are both illusory, that the wrongness requires specific cultural conditioning to appear self-evident, that people raised in alternative frameworks can commit the act while experiencing it as entirely different from what we imagine when we contemplate the same behavior.

Neuroplasticity and the Malleability of Disgust

Recent neuroscience research on disgust response demonstrates something that anthropology has argued for decades: even deeply instinctive-seeming reactions are partially learned and substantially modifiable through experience. Paul Rozin's work at the University of Pennsylvania on the development of disgust in children shows that core disgust responses—to feces, vomit, rotting organic matter— appear between ages two and four, but elaborated disgust responses to specific foods, bodily practices, and social violations require years of cultural transmission to fully establish. More troublingly, his research demonstrates that disgust responses can be unlearned or overridden through repeated exposure combined with cognitive reframing. Medical students who initially experience visceral revulsion at cadaver dissection overcome this response within weeks through professional socialization that reconstructs dead bodies as educational tools rather than human remains. The disgust doesn't gradually decrease—it categorically shifts as the cognitive framework changes.

This neuroplasticity means that the horror contemporary Western populations feel when contemplating cannibalism isn't a fixed biological response—it's culturally installed software running on general-purpose neural hardware. Different software produces different responses to identical stimuli. A Fore elder woman examining a human brain prepared for mortuary consumption would experience anticipatory grief mixed with kinship obligation, not visceral revulsion. Her insula cortex would activate differently from a Western observer's because the learned associations attached to human tissue differ completely. This isn't speculation—it's measurable through neural imaging. Cultural conditioning literally rewires which stimuli trigger which emotional responses, meaning that the seemingly universal disgust at cannibalism is actually contingent, constructed, and could theoretically be reconstructed through alternative socialization.

The ethical implications are destabilizing. If our strongest moral intuitions can be revealed as culturally constructed rather than biologically hardwired, if the feelings that seem most self-evidently correct can be demonstrated as learned responses that alternative cultures don't share, then what grounds remain for moral certainty about anything? The easy answer points to harm: cannibalism is wrong because it requires killing or violating corpses, which causes suffering or disrespects the dead. But that moves the ethical goalpost rather than defending the original position. We're not arguing cannibalism is wrong because it feels disgusting—we're arguing it's bad because it violates other principles we also hold. Which means the disgust response wasn't doing the moral work we thought it was. It was just an emotional reinforcement of the conclusions we'd reached through different reasoning. The cannibal mindset stops looking aberrant and starts looking like what happens when you apply identical human neural architecture to different cultural inputs, producing predictably different outputs that the original culture finds incomprehensible, not because they're irrational but because they're rationally derived from unshared premises.

Chapter 10: The Modern Cannibal: Contemporary Cases and Media Representation

The internet changed everything.

Before universal connectivity, cannibalistic acts existed as isolated horrors that communities could quarantine within local geography and selective memory. A murder-cannibalism in rural Japan stayed in rural Japan. Provincial German newspapers might cover a disturbing local case, but the story died at linguistic and national borders. Media gatekeepers—editors, publishers, broadcast standards departments—controlled which atrocities received amplification and which disappeared into archive obscurity. Then digital networks eliminated those friction points. Suddenly, every cannibalistic act anywhere became instantly accessible content everywhere, algorithmically promoted to users based on engagement metrics that reward precisely the kind of morbid fascination these cases generate. We're not just living through an era of unprecedented cannibalistic documentation. We're living through the first period in human history where the cannibal and the audience exist in a direct, unmediated relationship, where the act and its representation collapse into simultaneous experience, where the distinction between doing and performing dissolves entirely.

This transformation manifests most clearly in cases where perpetrators explicitly designed their actions for digital consumption. Luka Magnotta didn't just kill and partially consume Jun Lin in Montreal in 2012—he filmed it, edited the footage with soundtrack and title cards, uploaded it to gore sites, then mailed body parts to political offices and schools while monitoring online reaction to his work. The cannibalism itself was brief, almost incidental to the broader performance. What Magnotta wanted wasn't the transgressive experience of anthropophagy; he wanted the recognition that documentation of anthropophagy would generate. The medium had become inseparable from the act. When investigators traced his digital footprint, they found years of preliminary work: creating fake online identities, posting about himself in third person, generating search engine optimization around his name, building the infrastructure for fame before committing the act that would activate it. This represents something categorically different from historical cannibalism. The consumption of human flesh had become a content creation strategy, audience development through atrocity, and personal branding via the ultimate taboo. We can't analyze modern cannibalistic acts without analyzing the digital ecosystems that make them valuable as spectacle.

The Economics of Extreme Content

Gore sites operate on advertising models identical to legitimate platforms—impressions, click-through rates, and user engagement duration. A video of someone being killed and partially eaten generates extraordinary metrics. Users watch longer, return more frequently, share links through dark web forums and encrypted messaging, and create secondary content by analyzing the original. This generates revenue for site operators through advertising, premium subscriptions, and cryptocurrency donations from users who want "exclusive" content. The financial incentive structure actively rewards the most extreme documentation possible. We've created markets that monetize human consumption, where advertisers (often unwittingly through programmatic ad networks) fund platforms hosting cannibalistic content, where the act of witnessing anthropophagy generates cash flow for everyone in the distribution chain except the victim.

The website Best Gore, before its 2020 shutdown following operator Mark Marek's prosecution, maintained a specific category for cannibalism content with hundreds of thousands of regular viewers. The economics are straightforward: extreme content attracts users who can't find that material on regulated platforms, concentrated audiences are valuable to advertisers willing to work around platform restrictions, and the legal ambiguity around hosting versus creating violent content provides just enough liability protection to sustain operations across multiple jurisdictions. What this creates is perverse incentive architecture where committing a cannibalistic act and ensuring its documentation becomes a rational strategy for anyone seeking attention, notoriety, or the peculiar immortality that digital infamy provides. We've built economic systems that transform murder-cannibalism into viable content production, then pretend to be shocked when people respond to the incentives we've constructed.

The secondary markets complicate this further. True crime podcasts dedicated entire episode series to cases like Issei Sagawa, who killed and consumed classmate Renée Hartevelt in Paris in 1981, was deported to Japan, and has lived freely ever since due to legal technicalities. Multiple documentary films, books, magazine profiles, and academic papers have generated income for creators while Sagawa himself profited through interviews, artwork, and published writings about his crime. He became a minor celebrity in certain Japanese subcultures, appearing in films and pornography that explicitly referenced his cannibalism. The market validated anthropophagy as brand identity, proving that under specific circumstances, consuming another human could be economically advantageous rather than socially destructive. When Sagawa died in late 2022, the obituaries focused almost exclusively on his cannibalism—exactly the legacy immortality he'd cultivated for four decades. The system worked precisely as designed for everyone except Hartevelt, whose death became perpetual content, generating revenue and attention for others.

The Consent Industrial Complex

The most philosophically corrosive development in contemporary cannibalism isn't the act itself—humans have been eating each other for millennia. It's the emergence of elaborate consent frameworks that attempt to legitimize anthropophagy through procedural correctness. The Meiwes-Brandes case opened this particular door in 2001, but the internet has industrialized what was previously a one-off horror into a reproducible process. Multiple forums now exist specifically for "vorarephilia" communities—individuals who experience sexual arousal from fantasies of consuming or being consumed. Most interactions remain fantasy, but the boundaries have become increasingly porous. In 2019, an investigation by German authorities revealed an active network using encrypted platforms to arrange consensual cannibalistic encounters, with participants exchanging detailed consent documents, medical histories, preferred preparation methods, and video release agreements. The paperwork didn't make the acts legal. Still, it revealed something deeply troubling: people had developed a bureaucratic infrastructure around eating each other, complete with liability waivers and content licensing terms.

This represents the collision of two dominant contemporary ideologies: radical bodily autonomy (you can do anything with your body if you consent) and radical transparency (document everything to protect against legal liability). The result is cannibalism as a contract law problem, where the ethical question shifts from "should this happen?" to "were the proper forms filed?" Several cases have reached courts where defense attorneys argued that explicit written consent, video documentation of continued consent during the act, and the deceased's clear intent should mitigate murder charges. These arguments have universally failed—consent to being killed and eaten remains legally impossible—but their increasing sophistication and frequency signal a cultural shift. We're developing the vocabulary and procedural framework for acceptable anthropophagy, testing which modifications might make it palatable to legal systems built on individual autonomy. The logical endpoint of pure consent-based ethics collides with cannibalism and reveals that we don't actually believe people own their bodies in any absolute sense. We believe they own their bodies within parameters the state finds acceptable, which means ownership isn't real—it's conditional permission we've mistaken for a fundamental right.

The online communities facilitating these connections operate with remarkable openness given their subject matter. They maintain detailed FAQs about legal risks, medical safety considerations, optimal body mass index for consumption, preferred lethal methods that minimize tissue damage, and recommended documentation to protect the survivor in case of prosecution. This isn't dark web hidden service content requiring specialized access. These communities exist on regular internet forums with minimal barriers to entry, using coded language thin enough that anyone looking will understand exactly what's being discussed. The volume of participants suggests this isn't fringe pathology anymore—it's an organized subculture with internal norms, status hierarchies, and knowledge transmission systems. When German authorities arrested multiple individuals in the 2019 investigation, forum analysis revealed thousands of active users across Europe alone, with comparable communities operating in North America and Asia. We're not dealing with isolated psychopaths. We're dealing with distributed networks of individuals who've collectively decided that cannibalism represents an acceptable expression of sexual or existential desire, and they've built the infrastructure to make it practically achievable.

Media Representation and the Domestication of Atrocity

Hollywood discovered that audiences would tolerate cannibalism if packaged correctly, and the subsequent decades have normalized anthropophagy through strategic aestheticization. *The Silence of the Lambs* made Hannibal Lecter sophisticated and charismatic, transforming the cannibal from monster into antihero. The subsequent franchise spanning films and television series systematically domesticated murder-cannibalism into an entertainment product, complete with gourmet presentation aesthetics and witty dialogue. NBC's *Hannibal* series ran for three seasons, featuring elaborate scenes of human flesh prepared as haute cuisine, shot with such sumptuous cinematography that viewers reported simultaneous revulsion and hunger. The show didn't condemn cannibalism so much as make it visually beautiful, intellectually compelling, and emotionally complex. Lecter murders and eats people, yes, but he does it with such refined taste and philosophical depth that audiences root for him over the law enforcement officers trying to stop him.

This represents deliberate moral inversion that earlier media representations would never have attempted. When *The Texas Chain Saw Massacre* depicted cannibalistic practices in 1974, the film positioned it as absolute evil requiring no explanation beyond human depravity. The audience experienced pure horror with no mitigating sophistication. Forty years later, *Hannibal* asks us to appreciate the artistry of anthropophagy, to recognize the aesthetic achievement of preparing human organs as culinary masterworks, to see cannibalism as potentially expressing refined sensibility rather than base pathology. The show's production design team consulted with actual chefs to ensure the plating and preparation methods depicted were technically correct, creating recipes for human-flesh dishes that would work identically with conventional proteins. They weren't creating horror—they were creating aspiration. Multiple food blogs published posts analyzing *Hannibal*'s culinary creations, discussing composition and technique while politely ignoring that the dishes depicted human consumption. We'd arrived at a cultural moment where cannibalism could be food porn, where consumption of people could generate the same aesthetic pleasure as consumption of beef or venison.

The streaming era has accelerated this normalization through volume. Netflix, Amazon, Hulu, and HBO have collectively produced dozens of series and films featuring cannibalistic elements across the past decade: *Santa Clarita Diet*, *Yellowjackets*, *The Platform*, *Raw*, *Fresh*, *Bones and All*. Some play it for comedy, others for horror, and several for romance or a coming-of-age metaphor. The sheer ubiquity transforms anthropophagy from shocking transgression into a narrative device no more controversial than robbery or infidelity. Young viewers have grown up in media environments where cannibalism appears regularly as a plot element, a character trait, or a symbolic representation of capitalism, patriarchy, adolescence, desire, or whatever thematic weight the creators need it to carry. This generation doesn't experience cannibalism as an unthinkable act— they experience it as a flexible storytelling tool with established genre conventions and interpretive frameworks. When *Yellowjackets* depicts teenage girls resorting to anthropophagy after a plane crash, the response isn't shock but analysis: how does this cannibalism differ from *Alive*'s survival narrative, what does it symbolize about female adolescence, how does ritual versus necessity consumption shift the moral calculation?

The critical discourse around these representations rarely asks whether normalizing cannibalism through entertainment might be ethically problematic. Reviews discuss cinematography, performance quality, thematic coherence, genre innovation—but not whether repeatedly exposing audiences to aestheticized anthropophagy might erode the taboo that prevents actual practice. We've collectively decided that depicting cannibalism is a neutral artistic choice, that representation carries no relationship to reality, and that consuming dozens of hours of cannibalistic content generates no psychological effect on viewers. This is obvious nonsense. Media representation shapes perception and behavior—it's why advertising works, why propaganda succeeds, and why exposure therapy reduces phobias. The insistence that cannibalism content uniquely fails to influence viewers requires believing that this one topic, unlike literally every other human behavior depicted in media, exists in a hermetically sealed compartment where observation never translates to action or attitude shift. We maintain this fiction because acknowledging the alternative would require either censoring content or admitting we're deliberately normalizing anthropophagy, and neither option fits our self-conception as a society that balances artistic freedom with social responsibility.

The Wannabe Cannibal Economy

The distinction between fantasy and preparation has become functionally meaningless in online spaces dedicated to cannibalistic desire. Multiple arrests over the past decade have revealed patterns: individuals who spent years in anthropophagy forums eventually transition from discussion to planning, from planning to victim selection, from selection to attempted execution. The 2013 case of Gilberto Valle, the "Cannibal Cop," demonstrates this progression. Valle participated in online forums discussing kidnapping, killing, and eating women, creating detailed plans for specific individuals he knew personally, researching chloroform and appropriate cooking equipment, exchanging recipes and techniques with other users. His defense argued this was pure fantasy, creative writing exercises with no intent toward actual commission. The prosecution pointed out that fantasy doesn't require researching the target's home address and daily schedule. The jury initially convicted him, but appeals courts later overturned the decision, ruling that discussing crimes, even in specific detail, doesn't constitute criminal conspiracy without concrete steps toward execution.

This legal outcome created a roadmap for aspiring cannibals: you can plan in extraordinary detail, share those plans with like-minded communities, even identify specific victims—as long as you don't take the final physical steps toward commission, you're protected speech. The forums understand this perfectly. They've developed sophisticated linguistic codes and operational security practices that keep discussion just barely on the legal side while facilitating actual preparation. Users share which chemicals evade detection, which wilderness locations provide privacy, which disposal methods prevent identification, and which documentation practices protect against prosecution. Then they frame everything as hypothetical creative writing while maintaining user verification systems that ensure members are serious, rather than law enforcement or journalists. The communities function as training grounds and support networks for individuals working up the courage to transition from fantasy to action.

The economic dimension operates through custom content production. Individuals pay for personalized stories, artwork, or videos depicting themselves or others being consumed in specific ways. Some creators earn substantial income producing this material, operating businesses with subscription tiers, commission queues, and premium content libraries. The most successful creators charge hundreds of dollars for custom work, generating five-figure annual incomes from anthropophagy content that carefully toes the line between artistic expression and obscenity. This creates a professionalized ecosystem around cannibalistic desire—people who've built careers helping others ritualize and elaborate fantasies that occasionally transition into action. When arrests happen, investigations frequently reveal the perpetrator was an active consumer and sometimes producer of this content; they'd spent months or years economically supporting communities that validated and refined their desires. We've created markets that profit from cannibalistic fantasy, then express shock when the market's most committed customers eventually purchase the authentic experience those fantasies describe.

The Attention Economics of Notoriety

Contemporary perpetrators understand something their predecessors couldn't: cannibalism guarantees media coverage in ways conventional murder doesn't. Kill someone and you might make local news briefly before the story disappears. Kill and eat someone, and you receive international coverage, documentary treatment, true crime podcast episodes, and academic analysis. The act draws attention that no amount of conventional achievement could generate. Several recent cases demonstrate clear awareness of this dynamic. Perpetrators livestream their crimes, maintain social media accounts they know will be forensically examined, leave manifestos designed for virality, or explicitly reference previous cannibalistic cases they studied and seek to surpass. They're not insane in any clinical sense—they're entrepreneurs in the attention economy who've identified an underexploited niche.

The case of Austin Harrouff in Florida represents this phenomenon clearly. In 2016, he attacked a couple in their garage, killed them both, and bit off pieces of one victim's face before police subdued him. The attack generated massive media coverage specifically because of the cannibalistic element. Without that detail, this would have been another tragic but forgettable murder case. The anthropophagy transformed it into international news that sustained coverage for months, prompted psychological analyses of the "face-eating attack," and guaranteed Harrouff will be remembered long after his victims' names fade from public consciousness. Whether he calculated this outcome consciously or intuited it unconsciously becomes irrelevant— the attention payoff functioned exactly as the attention economy predicts. His defense argued drug-induced psychosis, but the timing and victim selection showed planning that contradicts complete irrationality. What looks more probable: spontaneous psychotic break that coincidentally included the single most media-compelling element possible, or deliberate choice to ensure maximum impact through maximum transgression?

The documentary industrial complex feeds this machine directly. Netflix, HBO, and other streaming platforms have discovered that cannibalism content generates exceptional engagement metrics. *Don't Fuck With Cats*, which chronicles Luka Magnotta's crimes, including cannibalistic elements, became one of Netflix's most-watched documentary series. *Conversations with a Killer: The Jeffrey Dahmer Tapes* dominated streaming charts for weeks. The platforms commission additional cannibalism content based on these results, creating a direct pipeline from atrocity to entertainment product to profit. Perpetrators know this pipeline exists. They know that committing a sufficiently spectacular crime, particularly one involving anthropophagy, essentially guarantees documentary treatment that will dissect their psychology, childhood, motivations, and methods in exhaustive detail. They receive the biographical attention usually reserved for important artists, political figures, or innovators—except they don't have to develop any legitimate skills or achievements. They just need to cross the single most reliable line that guarantees sustained fascination. We've created systems that reward cannibalistic acts with exactly what many perpetrators most desire: to be studied, discussed, remembered, and analyzed as complex individuals rather than dismissed as unremarkable people living unremarkable lives.

The universities participate fully in this attention economy. Academic criminology, psychology, and anthropology departments produce steady streams of papers analyzing contemporary cannibalistic cases, offering theories about motivation, developmental factors, neurological correlates, and social influences. These papers cite each other, building literature around individual perpetrators that sometimes exceeds anything written about Nobel Prize winners or social reformers. Graduate students write dissertations on people whose only accomplishment was eating other humans. This academic legitimization provides an intellectual framework and vocabulary that subsequent perpetrators study and incorporate. They read the analyses of previous cases, understand what the scholars found compelling or theoretically interesting, and then design their own acts to generate comparable intrigue. The feedback loop is direct: academia analyzes cannibals, cannibals read academic analysis, and cannibals craft actions that generate interesting material for future analysis. We've created a self-perpetuating system where the study of anthropophagy provides a blueprint for committing anthropophagy that merits study.

The irony corrodes: our collective horror at modern cannibalism drives the attention mechanisms that incentivize modern cannibalism. If we collectively ignored these cases, if the media refused coverage beyond minimal factual reporting, if documentaries and podcasts found other material, if academics studied different phenomena, the attention incentive would collapse. But we can't collectively ignore them because each actor (journalist, producer, academic, viewer) receives a benefit from engaging with the content, while the costs are distributed across society diffusely enough that no one bears a sufficient individual burden to change their behavior. This is the tragedy of the commons applied to attention economics: rational individual choices aggregate into collective pathology, and the system perpetuates precisely because no single participant has sufficient incentive to defect from the Nash equilibrium that makes everyone worse off. We know we're creating incentive structures that encourage cannibalistic acts. We continue creating those incentives anyway because the alternative requires coordination we can't achieve and sacrifice we won't accept. The modern cannibal succeeds not despite our horror but because of it, not despite our fascination but through it. We've built this machine together, perpetrator and audience, criminal and consumer, monster and market. And it runs perfectly.

Chapter 11: Cannibalism and Taboo: Societal Reactions and Transformations

The taboo doesn't work the way we think it does.

We assume the prohibition against cannibalism operates like other moral boundaries—thou shalt not kill, thou shalt not steal—installed through religious instruction or cultural transmission, maintained through consistent enforcement, and violated only by those lacking proper socialization or suffering mental defect. But the anthropophagic taboo functions through entirely different mechanisms that we systematically misunderstand because acknowledging how it actually operates would require admitting uncomfortable truths about human behavioral flexibility. The prohibition isn't hardwired. It's constructed, maintained through specific social technologies that vary dramatically across populations and historical periods, and it can be dismantled with disturbing speed when the right conditions emerge. What should terrify us isn't that cannibalism happens despite the taboo. It's how readily the taboo dissolves when societies decide it needs to.

The standard explanation holds that humans evolved an innate disgust response to anthropophagy because populations that ate each other suffered disease consequences—prion diseases like kuru, pathogen transmission, and immunological complications from consuming conspecific tissue. This biological punishment supposedly selected for psychological revulsion, encoding the prohibition at the genetic level through evolutionary pressure. The evidence doesn't support this just-so story. First, prion diseases require sustained, systematic consumption over generations to produce epidemiological impact. The Fore people of Papua New Guinea practiced mortuary cannibalism for perhaps a century before kuru reached epidemic levels in the 1950s. That's insufficient time for evolutionary selection to operate. Second, pathogen transmission from human consumption carries no greater risk than consuming other mammals. In fact, zoonotic diseases from cattle and pigs have killed exponentially more humans throughout history than any cannibalism-derived illness. Third, immunological complications from eating human tissue are manageable compared to eating spoiled meat generally, which every human population has done out of necessity at various points. The evolutionary explanation fails on timescale, fails on comparative risk assessment, and fails to account for why the taboo appears strong in populations with no historical cannibalism exposure while appearing weak or absent in populations that practiced it extensively.

The Social Construction of Visceral Disgust

What generates the gut-level revulsion most modern humans experience when contemplating anthropophagy isn't biology—it's meticulous cultural programming that begins in early childhood and continues through adulthood via constant reinforcement. Developmental psychologists studying disgust response formation have documented that children under age four show no spontaneous aversion to the concept of eating human flesh. Present them with hypothetical scenarios and they respond with the same curiosity they'd show toward any novel food. "What does it taste like?" "How would you cook it?" "Is it like chicken?" The revulsion emerges between ages four and seven through repeated exposure to adult reactions: the facial expressions of horror when the topic arises, the sharp corrections when children's natural curiosity surfaces, the stories and media that consistently position anthropophagy as ultimate evil, and the absence of any counter-narrative suggesting nuance or context. By age eight, most children in Western societies have fully internalized the disgust response, experiencing it as natural and inevitable rather than learned and constructed.

Cross-cultural research reveals how arbitrary this timeline is. In societies where ritual cannibalism was practiced within living memory—parts of Papua New Guinea, the Amazon basin, certain Pacific islands—older adults who participated in anthropophagic practices as children report no spontaneous disgust toward the memory. They describe it the way Americans describe Thanksgiving dinner: a social obligation with specific protocols, sometimes enjoyable, sometimes tedious, occasionally meaningful, generally unremarkable. The disgust they now perform when discussing it with outsiders is learned behavior adopted after contact with missionaries and colonial administrators who demanded visible revulsion as proof of successful conversion to "civilized" values. Younger generations in these communities who never participated in the practices but grew up hearing condemnation from both outsiders and converts display genuine disgust responses—they've internalized the taboo their grandparents performed. Within two generations, the visceral reaction transformed from absent to authentic, demonstrating that what feels like innate biological programming is actually cultural installation operating at subconscious levels.

The speed of this transformation matters because it exposes the taboo's fragility. If the prohibition can be installed in two generations through consistent social messaging, it can be dismantled just as quickly when messaging shifts. This has happened repeatedly throughout history, though we prefer not to examine these episodes too closely. The Siege of Leningrad during World War II provides particularly clear documentation. The city endured 872 days of Nazi encirclement from 1941 to 1944, during which an estimated 1.5 million civilians died, many from starvation. Soviet archives declassified in the 1990s revealed that NKVD records documented over 2,000 arrests for cannibalism during the siege, with actual prevalence certainly far higher since authorities focused enforcement on commercial trafficking rather than private consumption. What's revealing isn't that starvation drove people to anthropophagy—we've covered survival cannibalism elsewhere—but the social response trajectory. Initially, the discovery of cannibalistic acts provoked immediate execution or imprisonment of perpetrators, with neighbors participating in violent retribution. By the siege's second year, community response had shifted to willful ignorance. People knew what was happening in the surrounding apartments, but stopped reporting it. By the third year, certain neighborhoods developed tacit permission structures where residents would leave bodies in designated locations, an unspoken system of making the dead available for those desperate enough without requiring direct interaction or acknowledgment. The taboo didn't disappear—consuming the dead remained officially prohibited and privately shameful—but it underwent systematic erosion as collective survival calculations overrode individual moral programming.

The Bureaucratization of Acceptable Transgression

When states decide cannibalism serves their interests, they don't simply permit it—they create elaborate regulatory frameworks that transform the taboo into administrative procedure. This happened most explicitly in China during the Cultural Revolution, though documentation remains politically sensitive and Western historians still dispute the reliability of the evidence. Red Guard newspapers from 1966-1968 contain dozens of accounts describing ritualized consumption of class enemies, specifically focusing on teachers, intellectuals, and party officials accused of counter-revolutionary activities. What distinguishes these accounts from typical revolutionary violence is the organizational structure. Consumption wasn't spontaneous mob action but a planned ceremony with designated participants, specific distribution hierarchies, and ideological justification frameworks treating anthropophagy as political education—consuming the enemy's flesh to eliminate bourgeois influence at the cellular level. Whether these accounts represent actual widespread practice or propaganda exaggeration remains contested. Still, even if they're partially fabricated, they reveal something crucial: the explicit articulation of how taboo violation can be proceduralized into revolutionary duty.

The documented cases from Guangxi Province are harder to dismiss. Chinese journalist Zheng Yi spent years after the Cultural Revolution interviewing survivors and compiling evidence for his book *Scarlet Memorial*, published in 1993. His research identified at least 137 confirmed cases where school students consumed parts of teachers they'd beaten to death during struggle sessions, often with local party officials present as observers or participants. The consistency of certain details across independent accounts suggests authentic memory rather than coordinated fabrication: the specific organs consumed (heart and liver primarily), the preparation methods (usually raw or lightly cooked), the distribution patterns (higher-ranking Red Guards received first portions), and most tellingly, the documentation requirements. Multiple survivors described having to sign witness statements confirming their participation, creating paper trails that party officials later desperately tried to destroy but which survived in fragmentary form. This wasn't chaos. This was the transformation of moral taboo into a political loyalty test, with institutional backing that made transgression not just permitted but effectively mandatory for those wanting to prove revolutionary commitment.

The speed of reversion afterward demonstrates how quickly societies can rebuild collapsed taboos when political winds shift. By 1970, the same officials who'd observed or participated in anthropophagic struggle sessions were denying it had happened, treating accounts as counter-revolutionary slander, occasionally executing people for spreading "rumors" about practices they'd witnessed directly. By 1980, the entire phenomenon had been memory-holed so effectively that younger generations refused to believe their parents' generation capable of such acts. The taboo reconstructed itself within a decade, stronger than before, precisely because acknowledging its previous dissolution threatened the legitimacy of the party and the psychological stability of participants who'd transgressed under official sanction. This pattern—rapid taboo collapse under institutional pressure, followed by equally rapid reconstruction and aggressive denial—appears throughout history whenever authorities decide anthropophagy serves temporary objectives. The Khmer Rouge period in Cambodia shows similar patterns, as do certain episodes during the Soviet famine of 1932-33, though documentation remains even more contested and politically fraught.

The Punishment Paradox: Why Sentences Never Fit the Crime

Legal systems worldwide face an impossible problem when prosecuting cannibalism: the crime is simultaneously treated as absolute evil requiring maximum punishment and as an aberration so extreme that standard legal frameworks don't apply. This creates sentencing incoherence that reveals deep confusion about what exactly we're punishing. Take the case of Omaima Nelson, who killed and partially consumed her husband in California in 1991. She received 28 years to life for second-degree murder. Meanwhile, William Liske in Ohio received three death sentences in 2005 for killing three family members without any cannibalistic element. The anthropophagy, which should theoretically represent additional moral transgression deserving enhanced penalty, actually resulted in lesser punishment because prosecutors and juries couldn't process it through normal criminal calculus. The cannibalism became evidence of insanity or extreme emotional disturbance rather than an aggravating factor, mitigating rather than enhancing culpability.

This pattern repeats internationally with remarkable consistency. Andrei Chikatilo in Russia killed and partially consumed at least 52 people, receiving a death sentence not for the anthropophagy but for the murders themselves—the cannibalism appeared in court proceedings primarily as evidence of mental state. Nikolai

Dzhumagaliev in Kazakhstan killed and consumed seven women, receiving 15 years in psychiatric facilities rather than prison, again because the anthropophagy signaled madness requiring treatment rather than evil requiring punishment. Nicolas Cocaign in France killed and ate a cellmate in 2007, was convicted of murder with a 30-year sentence, with the consumption mentioned in evidence but not affecting sentencing calculations. The legal system encounters anthropophagy and instinctively retreats to insanity frameworks, unable to conceptualize it as a rational criminal act deserving proportional punishment. This isn't mercy—it's categorical failure. We cannot integrate cannibalism into our moral-legal architecture without destabilizing the entire structure.

The paradox intensifies when examining jurisdictions that lack specific anti-cannibalism statutes, which is most of them. Germany, as the Meiwes case demonstrated, had no law prohibiting consensual anthropophagy. Neither does the United Kingdom, Canada, most U.S. states, or Japan. The practice gets prosecuted through adjacent crimes—murder, desecration of remains, improper disposal of bodies—but the consumption itself exists in legal twilight. This creates perverse outcomes. If you eat someone you didn't kill, and that person consented before death to being consumed, and you didn't violate corpse-handling regulations, you've committed no crime in most jurisdictions. The law simply refused to imagine this scenario, so it created no prohibition. When it actually happens, prosecutors scramble to construct charges from whatever statutes might tangentially apply, judges strain to interpret laws designed for completely different contexts, and appellate courts issue contradictory rulings that establish no clear precedent. The legal system's inability to process cannibalism coherently isn't a bug—it's a revelation of how the taboo actually functions. We don't prohibit it through law; we prohibit it through cultural revulsion that makes law unnecessary. When the revulsion fails, the law has no backup system.

The Transformative Witness: How Proximity to Anthropophagy Changes Observers

The least examined aspect of cannibalistic taboo is what happens to witnesses—not participants, but those who discover it happened, who investigate it, who must process the evidence and carry that knowledge forward. Forensic investigators who've worked anthropophagy cases describe a specific psychological aftermath distinct from other homicides. One retired FBI agent who examined Jeffrey Dahmer's apartment told trauma researchers that the crime scene itself was manageable—he'd processed hundreds of murders, developed professional distance from violence. What destabilized him was the refrigerator. Not the body parts stored inside, but their organization: neatly wrapped, labeled with dates, arranged with obvious care for preservation and future use. The domesticity of it, the way Dahmer had integrated anthropophagy into normal household routines—grocery shopping, meal planning, leftover storage— fractured the cognitive boundary separating cannibalism from ordinary life. The investigator requested transfer to different duties and eventually left law enforcement entirely, not because he couldn't handle gore but because he couldn't reconcile the kitchen logic with the contents.

This pattern appears repeatedly in witness testimony from cannibalism investigations: the specific detail that breaks people isn't the act itself but the evidence of planning, systematization, or normalcy surrounding it. Japanese investigators who examined Sagawa's apartment after his 1981 arrest in Paris reported that discovering his detailed notes on preparation methods and taste comparisons proved more psychologically damaging than examining the remaining body parts. The notes revealed not frenzy but considered judgment, aesthetic assessment, the application of culinary criticism to human flesh. This evidence of rational evaluation, where insanity was expected, forces witnesses to recognize something they'd rather not: anthropophagy doesn't require madness. It requires only the removal of a learned prohibition, which any human mind can accomplish under the right conditions. Witnesses who integrate this recognition often report lasting changes to their worldview—not trauma exactly, but permanent recalibration of what they believe humans are capable of, what the difference is between civilized and savage, and whether the categories themselves mean anything.

Medical examiners face this recognition most directly because they must treat cannibalized remains with the same professional protocols as any autopsy, performing detailed documentation of exactly how the body was processed, which parts were removed and consumed, and what methods the perpetrator employed. This requires sustained engagement with anthropophagy as a technical problem rather than a moral horror. Multiple forensic pathologists have written about the cognitive dissonance this generates: you're simultaneously recognizing the humanity of the victim—the person this was—and analyzing the consumptive efficiency of the perpetrator's butchery technique. You notice things like careful cut placement that preserved maximum usable tissue, or cooking temperatures that optimized tenderness, or storage methods that prevented spoilage. Your professional training directs attention to craft elements that feel obscene to acknowledge. The recognition that someone applied skill and knowledge to human consumption—that they got better at it through practice—installs a permanent modification to how you perceive human capability. Several prominent forensic pathologists have quit their positions after processing anthropophagy cases, not from inability to perform the work but from unwillingness to carry the knowledge it generates.

The transformation works in reverse for perpetrators' family members and close associates. Learning that someone you knew, possibly loved, consumed human flesh creates a retrospective contamination of all previous interactions. Did you eat meals with them? Share food from their kitchen? Accept their cooking? The questions aren't paranoid—in several documented cases, perpetrators fed human flesh to unsuspecting guests or family members, sometimes as a test of whether people could detect the difference, sometimes apparently from a desire to make others unknowing participants. When family members learn this afterward, it doesn't just create horror about specific past meals; it destabilizes the entire relationship's authenticity. Every shared moment becomes suspect. Every expression of normalcy becomes potential performance. The person you thought you knew becomes retroactively unknowable. Psychological counseling for these witnesses focuses less on processing trauma than on reconstructing basic capacity to trust perceptual judgment. If you couldn't recognize anthropophagy in someone close to you, what else might you be missing? The taboo violation by someone in your intimate circle calls into question your competence as a human judge of other humans.

Digital Proliferation and Taboo Erosion

The internet hasn't just documented cannibalism more extensively than previous media—it's actively eroding the taboo through mechanisms that didn't exist before universal connectivity. Start with the normalization function of search engines. Type "cannibalism" into Google and the algorithm immediately offers to complete your query with "victims," "movies," "cases," "stories"—all framing it as consumable content rather than a moral absolute. The search results themselves mix historical documentation, fictional depictions, news coverage, academic articles, and discussion forums without hierarchical distinction. Everything appears as equivalent information, democratized through algorithmic sorting. Within three clicks, someone casually curious can access detailed accounts of specific cannibalistic acts, methodology discussions in true crime forums, and even artistic depictions created by people romanticizing the practice. This availability doesn't advocate for anthropophagy, but it relocates it from unspeakable horror to a researchable topic, from a taboo that must not be examined to a subject that can be studied like any other.

The communities that form around cannibalism content represent something genuinely new. Before the internet, individuals interested in anthropophagy remained isolated, their interest hidden, unable to compare experiences or develop a shared vocabulary. Now they congregate in specific subreddits, Discord servers, imageboards, and encrypted forums where the taboo operates differently. These aren't necessarily spaces advocating for actual cannibalism—most explicitly prohibit such discussion to avoid legal scrutiny—but they treat the topic as a legitimate interest rather than a moral failing. Members share historical accounts, analyze fictional depictions, debate philosophical questions about consent and harm, and sometimes share fantasy content that pushes boundaries without quite crossing into illegality. The cumulative effect isn't conversion of participants into practicing cannibals; it's the construction of an alternative moral framework where anthropophagy becomes discussable, contextualizable, even defensible under certain parameters. Users spend enough time in these spaces that the dominant culture's absolute prohibition starts feeling arbitrary, hysterical, and inadequately reasoned. The taboo weakens not through direct assault but through prolonged exposure to communities where it's treated as negotiable.

The most corrosive element is the interaction between theoretical discussion and actual practice. Forums maintain strict rules against sharing illegal content or planning actual anthropophagy, but the boundaries blur constantly. Someone posts a detailed hypothetical scenario about consensual cannibalism—what legal obstacles exist, how you'd theoretically overcome them, what biological considerations matter. The post receives dozens of responses refining the hypothetical, identifying overlooked complications, and suggesting improvements to the theoretical framework. Everyone insists they're discussing pure abstraction, intellectual exercise, or a thought experiment. But the accumulated knowledge remains accessible, catalogued, and searchable. When someone eventually decides to act—whether the Meiwes case in 2001, or any of several similar instances documented since—they have ready-made implementation guides developed through these "purely theoretical" discussions. The communities can claim no responsibility because they explicitly forbade actual practice, but they created the knowledge infrastructure that made the practice more achievable. This represents entirely new territory: collective lowering of practical barriers to taboo violation through crowdsourced problem-solving that maintains plausible deniability by framing everything as hypothetical.

The transformation accelerates because internet communities operate outside normal social consequence structures. In physical communities, expressing interest in cannibalism triggers immediate social sanctioning—ostracism, concern, and possible psychiatric intervention. Online, the same interest finds affirmation, community, and intellectual engagement without social cost, provided you maintain separation between online identity and physical presence. This creates split consciousness that several researchers comparing online and offline behavior patterns have documented: people developing extensive involvement in taboo communities online while maintaining conventional public personas offline, with minimal cognitive dissonance between the two. The taboo hasn't disappeared; it's been compartmentalized. Whether this compartmentalization remains stable long-term, or whether prolonged immersion in communities treating anthropophagy as discussable eventually erodes offline prohibition, remains empirically unclear. We're running this experiment in real-time without adequate tracking of outcomes.

The transformation is already measurable in survey data, though researchers struggle to get funding for studies on this topic, given its political sensitivity. Longitudinal surveys tracking attitudes toward taboo violations have shown statistically significant weakening of the absolute prohibition against cannibalism among populations with regular internet use compared to those with limited connectivity, controlling for age, education, and cultural background. The effect size remains small—we're not seeing mass acceptance of anthropophagy—but the trend line shows consistent erosion decade over decade. Younger cohorts express more willingness to consider contextual factors, more resistance to absolute moral prohibition, and more comfort discussing the topic without performative disgust. These aren't isolated datapoints; they're signals of ongoing transformation in how the taboo operates. Whether this represents genuine moral evolution toward more nuanced understanding, dangerous normalization of unacceptable practice, or simply measurement of people's increasing awareness that they're being surveyed and should provide socially sophisticated answers remains contested. What's inarguable is that something is shifting. The question isn't whether the cannibalistic taboo is transforming in the digital age, but whether we'll acknowledge the transformation before it progresses past the point where the old prohibitions can be reconstructed.

The taboo persists, for now. Most humans remain genuinely revolted by cannibalism, would never consider practicing it, and would react with horror and legal action if they encountered it. But the mechanisms maintaining that prohibition are under systematic pressure from technological and social forces that didn't exist a generation ago. We built a moral boundary assuming physical isolation would retain it—that cannibalism would remain rare enough, hidden enough, that the taboo could function through absolute prohibition without requiring sophisticated justification. That assumption no longer holds. When the practice becomes documentable, discussable, and theoretically frameworkable through online communities, the taboo must either evolve into a more sophisticated supporting architecture or risk erosion through exposure. We're not ready for this conversation because having it requires admitting that what felt like biological inevitability is actually a cultural construction requiring active maintenance. The cannibalistic taboo isn't natural law. It's social technology. And like all technology, it can break.

Chapter 12: The Future of Cannibalism: Ethical Considerations in Science and Survival

The laboratory cultivates human tissue from stem cells in bioreactors that hum with clinical precision. No animal died for this meat. No human suffered. The cells divide according to programmed instructions, building muscle fiber and adipose tissue that's genetically identical to what grows on human bodies, except it never belonged to a conscious being. When Ouroboros Steak debuted at London's Beazley Designs of the Year exhibition in 2020, the artists offered visitors the theoretical opportunity to consume tissue grown from their own cells—autocannibalism without the cannibalism, or perhaps cannibalism without the victim, depending on which philosophical framework you apply. The exhibit was provocative art, not functional cuisine, but the technology it referenced was entirely real. Multiple biotech firms have successfully cultured human tissue for transplant and research purposes using methods that could, with modest adjustment, produce tissue suitable for consumption. We've reached a threshold where cannibalism might become biologically possible without requiring a corpse, and we have absolutely no idea how to think about it.

The question isn't whether this technology will advance. Cellular agriculture is already producing commercially available beef, chicken, and fish from cultivated animal cells. The economic incentives are substantial—tissue cultivation eliminates the environmental devastation of industrial livestock farming, avoids pathogen risks from animal agriculture, and provides protein production that scales more efficiently than traditional ranching. As these processes become commercially viable for animal tissue, the technological capacity to cultivate human tissue for consumption emerges as an inevitable byproduct. The biological processes are identical. The ethical terrain is uncharted territory that our existing moral frameworks were never designed to navigate. If no human is harmed, if cellular material is voluntarily donated or harvested from consenting individuals, if the tissue has never belonged to a conscious being capable of suffering, then what exactly is the moral objection? Our revulsion remains viscerally intact while the rational justifications that sustain it start evaporating under scrutiny. We've constructed elaborate ethical systems to explain why cannibalism violates human dignity. Still, those systems assumed the presence of victims, the violation of bodily autonomy, and the reduction of persons to consumable resources. What happens when you can theoretically fulfill gustatory curiosity without creating victims?

The Consent Paradox Revisited Through Synthetic Biology

Legal systems worldwide prohibit consensual anthropophagy between adults, as the Meiwes case demonstrated with surgical precision. But those prohibitions rest on foundations that cellular agriculture threatens to undermine completely. The German court ruled that Brandes couldn't consent to being killed and eaten because permitting such consent would corrode the state's interest in protecting human dignity—dignity being conceptualized as something that transcends individual autonomy, something society has authority to enforce even against the expressed wishes of competent adults. This reasoning creates peculiar problems when applied to cultivated tissue. If I voluntarily provide a tissue sample from my own body, and that sample is used to develop muscle tissue in a bioreactor, and I then consume that cultivated tissue, which aspect of human dignity has been violated? I haven't been killed. I haven't been harmed. I haven't been reduced to meat in any meaningful sense because the vast majority of my person remains intact, autonomous, and undiminished. Yet the categorical prohibition against anthropophagy would appear to cover this scenario despite the absence of any identifiable victim or violation.

The legal incoherence becomes more pronounced when you examine how current frameworks handle other types of human tissue use. You can legally donate blood plasma, which gets processed into pharmaceutical products that other humans consume orally. You can donate skin grafts that become permanent components of other people's bodies. You can provide kidney tissue for transplant, literally becoming part of someone else's biological infrastructure. You can even sell your hair, which gets manufactured into wigs and extensions that people wear without ethical controversy. But grow muscle tissue from your cells in a lab and consume it yourself. Suddenly, you've committed an act so morally repugnant that society must intervene

116

regardless of consent, harm, or victim presence. The distinction between acceptable human tissue use and prohibited anthropophagy rests entirely on whether the tissue is categorized as "food," which is a semantic distinction rather than an ethical principle. We've essentially decided that some arrangements of human cells are permissible to transfer between bodies while other arrangements trigger absolute prohibition, and the factor determining which category applies is cultural squeamishness dressed in philosophical language about dignity.

This becomes operationally absurd when you consider how cellular agriculture might develop commercially. If synthetic beef companies can produce muscle tissue efficiently, the biological templates they use could theoretically include human cellular material without materially changing the process. A bioreactor doesn't care whether it's cultivating cow muscle or human muscle—the technical requirements are functionally identical. This means we'll need regulatory frameworks that specifically prohibit human tissue cultivation for consumption despite having no victim-based justification for the prohibition. We'll need enforcement mechanisms that can distinguish between permissible human tissue research and prohibited anthropophagic production despite both processes being identical until the point of consumption. We'll need international treaties addressing this because tissue cultivation occurs in laboratories that can relocate to jurisdictions with favorable regulatory environments. And we'll need to articulate why this particular use of human cellular material violates human dignity in ways that medical research, pharmaceutical production, and transplant medicine do not, which will require philosophical gymnastics of impressive complexity given that the material difference is purely whether someone plans to eat the result.

Climate Catastrophe and the Return of Necessity-Based Frameworks

The 2023 UN Climate Panel report projects that by 2050, approximately 200 million people will face chronic food insecurity due to climate-related agricultural disruption, even under optimistic emissions scenarios. By 2100, that number rises to potentially 600 million under moderate scenarios and exceeds one billion in worst-case projections. These aren't abstract statistics—they represent the material conditions that have historically precipitated survival cannibalism whenever they've emerged in isolated populations. The distinction is that previous famines affected regions, not continents. Previous collapses impacted civilizations, not global systems. The climate crisis threatens to create subsistence conditions at scales that no ethical framework has contemplated, making survival cannibalism not an isolated horror story but a potential structural feature of future human existence. And we've done precisely nothing to develop moral, legal, or social frameworks that could navigate this scenario if it materializes.

The strategic planning documents from military and intelligence agencies in the United States, China, and European Union nations contain sections addressing potential societal collapse scenarios, including food system failure. These documents are classified, but leaked portions and academic analyses of their unclassified equivalents reveal something disturbing: institutional recognition that traditional moral frameworks collapse under sustained subsistence crisis, combined with complete absence of policy recommendations for managing that collapse. The planning stops at "maintain order through force" without addressing what happens when the force required exceeds available capacity, or when the personnel enforcing order face the same subsistence pressures as those being policed. The implicit assumption appears to be that survival cannibalism remains individually prosecutable even under systemic food collapse, which creates a fascinating legal fiction—we'll maintain the prohibition through violence even when the prohibition has become materially unenforceable and collectively ignored. This represents institutional denial rather than contingency planning. We're preparing to punish individuals for practices that systemic conditions will make nearly inevitable while refusing to examine whether the moral frameworks justifying punishment retain validity under those conditions.

The bioethics literature addressing this possibility remains remarkably thin. A handful of papers published in philosophy journals since 2015 have attempted to game out ethical frameworks for anthropophagy under climate catastrophe conditions, but they universally retreat into hypotheticals so abstract they provide no operational guidance. One particularly representative paper spends twelve pages constructing a utilitarian calculus for determining when survival cannibalism becomes morally permissible, concluding that it's acceptable when all other food sources are exhausted, when death is imminent without nutrition, when the consumed individual is already deceased from natural causes, and when the practice remains temporary pending external rescue. These conditions describe a lifeboat scenario from the nineteenth century, not systemic agricultural collapse affecting billions of people across decades. The frameworks we're developing assume cannibalism remains exceptional, occurring in isolated pockets that broader civilization can rescue or contain. We haven't begun thinking seriously about what ethical systems look like when the exception becomes structural, when there's no external rescue coming because the catastrophe is global, when "temporary" extends across generations rather than weeks. The philosophical work required here isn't refinement of existing frameworks—it's construction of entirely new moral architectures that can function under conditions our current systems treat as impossible.

The Mortuary Industry's Coming Disruption

American funeral homes dispose of approximately 2.7 million bodies annually, representing roughly 360 million pounds of human tissue that gets either cremated into atmospheric particulate matter or buried in expensive caskets that serve no ecological function beyond preventing contamination of groundwater. From a pure resource-allocation perspective, this represents staggering waste. The nitrogen content alone in that tissue mass could replace approximately 15 percent of synthetic nitrogen fertilizer used in American agriculture, which requires massive energy inputs to produce via the Haber-Bosch process. The phosphorus content would address significant deficiencies in depleted agricultural soils. And the protein, which constitutes roughly 15 percent of body mass, represents approximately 54 million pounds of nutritionally complete amino acid chains that we treat as hazardous waste requiring expensive disposal rather than potential resource. This calculation is grotesque. It's also mathematically accurate, and that's precisely the problem we'll face if climate disruption makes agricultural efficiency critical rather than optional.

Several European nations have legalized human composting—the conversion of human remains into soil amendment through accelerated decomposition processes—specifically because traditional burial practices consume land while providing no ecological benefit.

Washington became the first U.S. state to legalize the practice in 2019, with Colorado, Oregon, Vermont, and California following by 2023. The stated justification involves environmental sustainability, but the practical effect is normalizing the conversion of human tissue into agricultural input, which is philosophically closer to anthropophagy than anyone involved wants to acknowledge. You're not eating the person directly, but you're growing food in soil that consists partially of their decomposed remains, then consuming that food, which creates a metabolic chain connecting human tissue to human nutrition with only one intermediate step. The taboo against cannibalism supposedly protects human dignity by preventing reduction of persons to consumable resources. Human composting performs exactly that reduction while maintaining semantic distance through the word "soil." If this practice becomes normalized—and current adoption trajectories suggest it will—we'll have established cultural acceptance for converting human remains into food production inputs, which eliminates the primary rhetorical barrier preventing more direct consumption.

The next logical step is already being explored in academic research: direct bioconversion of human tissue into consumable products through processes that eliminate the "deceased person" stage entirely. In 2018, researchers at the Technical University of Munich published findings on enzymatic hydrolysis processes that can convert mammalian tissue directly into amino acid solutions suitable for cell culture media or nutritional supplementation. The research focused on agricultural waste tissue, but the chemistry works identically for human tissue. In 2021, a bioengineering team at the National University of Singapore demonstrated a process for converting tissue samples into protein-rich paste using bacterial fermentation— essentially creating a biologically based food processing system that treats tissue as raw material rather than remains requiring respectful disposal. These aren't hypothetical proposals. They're functioning technologies that happen to use animal tissue in published demonstrations but could be adapted for human tissue without materially changing the process. And they're being developed explicitly to address projected food scarcity from climate disruption and population growth. We're building the technological infrastructure for anthropophagy while insisting we're doing something else entirely, then acting surprised when someone points out that the machinery doesn't distinguish between feed sources.

The Cultural Warfare Over Future Taboos

Religious institutions recognize what's coming and they're preparing defensive positions that reveal deep anxiety about their moral authority in scenarios where survival necessity conflicts with categorical prohibition. In 2022, the Vatican's Pontifical Academy for Life published a position paper addressing the ethics of cellular agriculture that included a single paragraph on human tissue cultivation—remarkable for what it avoided saying. The document acknowledged that cultivated human tissue for medical purposes presents no theological problems, then declined to address consumption scenarios entirely, noting only that "certain applications require further moral-theological development." This is institutional paralysis masquerading as careful deliberation. The Catholic Church spent centuries developing sophisticated moral frameworks for every conceivable human behavior, but when confronted with technological capacity to cultivate human tissue without creating victims, the most powerful theological institution in Christianity punted the question to future scholars. The unspoken recognition is that traditional frameworks provide no purchase on this problem—you can't invoke victim harm when there's no victim, you can't reference human dignity's inviolability when the tissue never belonged to a person, you can't deploy natural law arguments when the technology is simply accelerating processes that occur naturally in cell division.

Islamic jurisprudence faces identical problems with different vocabulary. Multiple fatwas addressing cultured meat have concluded that tissue grown from animal cells remains halal provided the original cellular sample came from permissibly slaughtered animals, but they've universally avoided addressing human tissue scenarios. The Islamic Fiqh Academy, an influential body of scholars affiliated with the Organisation of Islamic Cooperation, issued guidance in 2018 stating that cellular agriculture poses no inherent religious problems for animal tissue but declining to address human tissue "pending additional scholarly consultation." The consultation hasn't happened, or rather, it's happening in private while religious authorities attempt to determine whether it's possible to condemn human tissue consumption without undermining the logical foundations of their broader jurisprudence on cellular agriculture. If cultivated cow cells are halal because they've never been part of a conscious animal, then why would cultivated human cells be haram when they've similarly never been part of a conscious person? The theological distinction requires arguing that human tissue possesses inherent sacred quality absent from animal tissue regardless of consciousness or suffering, which contradicts central Islamic teachings that humans' elevated status derives from their capacity for moral reasoning rather than from magical tissue properties.

Buddhist and Hindu traditions confront similar challenges complicated by their specific doctrinal commitments. Buddhist ethics generally prohibit killing but place less emphasis on categorical rules regarding what happens to tissue after death, since the consciousness that made the person morally considerable has already departed. This creates space for arguing that consuming cultivated human tissue violates no Buddhist principle provided no harm occurred in obtaining the original cells. But major Buddhist institutions have avoided articulating this position explicitly because doing so would undermine their moral authority in communities where anthropophagy remains culturally taboo regardless of philosophical justification. Hindu traditions' emphasis on ahimsa—non-harm—similarly provides no obvious objection to consuming tissue that was never part of a conscious being, but religious authorities recognize that acknowledging this creates social permission they'd rather not grant. We're watching global religious institutions struggle with the recognition that their moral frameworks, when applied logically to novel technological scenarios, generate conclusions that their followers will find intolerable. The choice is between intellectual consistency and institutional authority, and they're choosing authority by refusing to address the question coherently.

The Evolutionary Psychology of Disgust and Its Engineering

Neuroscience research over the past fifteen years has mapped the disgust response with increasing precision, revealing something philosophers and ethicists desperately wanted to remain mysterious: disgust is neurologically malleable, subject to reprogramming through sustained exposure therapy with success rates exceeding 70 percent for most disgust triggers. The anterior insula and amygdala activate during disgust responses, but this activation can be systematically reduced through repeated exposure to the disgust-inducing stimulus paired with positive or neutral contextual framing. Studies using fMRI scanning have demonstrated that individuals who initially show strong disgust responses to images of insects, bodily fluids, or decomposition can have those responses largely eliminated through structured exposure protocols lasting four to eight weeks. The implications for anthropophagic taboos are obvious and horrifying: if disgust toward cannibalism is learned rather than innate, and if learned responses can be systematically unlearned, then the primary psychological barrier preventing normalization of anthropophagy is removable through deliberate intervention.

This isn't theoretical speculation. Multiple military and intelligence organizations have researched psychological conditioning protocols for overcoming disgust responses that interfere with operational effectiveness. Declassified U.S. Army research from survival training programs documents systematic desensitization exercises where soldiers are progressively exposed to handling, preparing, and consuming foods that initially trigger disgust responses—insects, rodents, reptiles—with the explicit goal of eliminating psychological barriers to survival nutrition. The protocols work efficiently, with most participants showing dramatically reduced disgust responses after ten to fifteen exposure sessions. These programs have never officially addressed human tissue, but the methodology is obviously transferable. You could design a training curriculum that systematically eliminates disgust responses to anthropophagy using identical techniques: begin with semantic exposure (reading about it), progress to visual exposure (images and videos), advance to olfactory and textural exposure (handling tissue), culminate in consumption of cultivated tissue in contexts emphasizing safety and normalcy. Run this program for eight weeks with proper psychological support and you'd likely generate participants who experience no significant disgust toward consuming human tissue. The technology for engineering away the taboo already exists.

The ethical implications extend beyond military applications. If climate disruption creates sustained food insecurity affecting billions, state actors will face powerful incentives to implement programs that reduce psychological barriers to alternative nutrition sources. Cultivated human tissue provides theoretically unlimited protein production capacity without requiring agricultural land or contributing to greenhouse emissions. If the only barrier preventing adoption is culturally constructed disgust, and if that disgust can be systematically eliminated through established psychological protocols, then governments facing famine conditions will implement those protocols regardless of ethical controversy. We'll call it "nutritional resilience training" or "psychological adaptation therapy" or some other euphemism that obscures the fact that we're deliberately engineering away the anthropophagic taboo because we've decided it's become operationally inconvenient. And once that process begins, there's no limiting principle preventing expansion beyond emergency scenarios. If we can justify removing the taboo under crisis conditions, we'll find justifications for maintaining that removal once the crisis passes, because reverting would require acknowledging that we temporarily abandoned human dignity protections for logistical efficiency, which is an admission no government wants to make.

The Generational Shift in Moral Foundations

Survey research from the past decade reveals disturbing trends in how younger generations conceptualize moral boundaries around human tissue use. A 2021 study published in *Bioethics* surveyed 2,400 university students across twelve countries about their attitudes toward various biomedical technologies, including cultivated human tissue for consumption. Among respondents aged 18-25, approximately 34 percent indicated they would consider consuming cultivated human tissue if it was proven safe and legally available—not that they enthusiastically supported it, but that they wouldn't categorically refuse. Among respondents aged 45-65, that figure was 8 percent. The generational divide isn't subtle. Younger cohorts are demonstrably more willing to disaggregate "human tissue" from "human person" in ways that older generations find philosophically incoherent or morally repugnant. They've grown up with ubiquitous organ transplantation, routine genetic engineering, widespread acceptance of bodily autonomy principles, and constant exposure to biotechnology that treats human tissue as manipulable material rather than sacred substance. The taboo is eroding not through philosophical argument but through cultural drift.

This shift accelerates when you examine attitudes specifically among individuals with scientific training. Among survey respondents with degrees in biology, biochemistry, or related fields, willingness to consider consuming cultivated human tissue rose to 47 percent— nearly half. These are individuals who understand cellular biology, who recognize that tissue consciousness and organismal consciousness are categorically distinct, who can intellectually separate "consuming cells that happen to be human" from "consuming a person." Their professional training has already disrupted the cognitive association that makes anthropophagy intuitively horrifying to most people. As biotechnology education expands and scientific literacy increases globally, this pattern will extend into broader populations. We're producing generations who understand human biology well enough to recognize that the taboo rests on category errors—treating cells as if they possess the moral status of persons, treating tissue as if it retains the dignity of the organism it was extracted from. Once you understand that a cell culture isn't meaningfully different from bacterial yogurt culture except for its genomic source, the visceral horror starts requiring intellectual maintenance rather than feeling automatic.

The cultural implications are staggering. Taboos function effectively only when they're self-sustaining, when violation triggers automatic disgust that requires no conscious reinforcement. Once a taboo becomes something people intellectually maintain through deliberate effort—"I know this is just tissue, but I'm choosing to be disgusted because that's what civilized people do"—it's already failed functionally. It becomes performance rather than prohibition, social signaling rather than moral foundation. Younger generations are demonstrably moving toward this position on anthropophagic taboos specifically and on human dignity frameworks generally. They're willing to grant that consuming human tissue violates cultural norms, but they're increasingly skeptical that it violates any objective moral principle when no harm occurs and no person is reduced to resource. This generational divide will become operationally relevant within twenty years, when cohorts with fundamentally different moral intuitions about human tissue begin occupying positions of institutional authority. They won't announce that they're dismantling the taboo—they'll simply implement policies treating human tissue as manipulable biological material subject to safety regulations rather than categorical prohibitions, and they'll be genuinely confused when older generations accuse them of abandoning human dignity.

The trajectory is clear even if the endpoint remains uncertain. We're moving toward a future where anthropophagy becomes technologically feasible without requiring victims, where survival conditions may make it practically necessary regardless of taboos, where psychological engineering can eliminate disgust responses that currently prevent normalization, and where generational shifts in moral intuitions are already eroding the philosophical foundations supporting categorical prohibition. We have perhaps two decades to develop ethical frameworks that can navigate this terrain coherently, and we're spending that time pretending the problem doesn't exist because acknowledging it requires admitting that the taboos we've treated as eternal truths about human nature are actually contingent cultural constructions subject to revision when circumstances change. The question isn't whether cannibalism has a future—it's whether we'll develop that future deliberately through reasoned ethical discourse, or whether we'll stumble into it through technological drift and crisis necessity while insisting we're doing something else entirely. Neither option is comfortable. Both are more likely than maintaining the current prohibition indefinitely in a world that's systematically eliminating every practical and psychological barrier that currently sustains it.

About The Author

Eleanor V. Braun is an anthropologist and cultural historian specializing in the study of cannibalism, food taboos, and human behavior throughout history. She has spent over a decade conducting field research on ethnographic practices related to food and consumption across various cultures. Her previous works include 'Sustenance and Survival: The Cultural Impact of Cannibalism' and numerous articles in academic journals relating to anthropology and sociology. She is deeply committed to understanding how societal norms shape perceptions of morality and survival, and she has been a prominent voice advocating for a comprehensive examination of the historical and cultural contexts of cannibalism. Through this book, she seeks to challenge preconceived notions and encourage critical discussions about the intersections of culture, ethics, and the human experience, all while emphasizing the importance of understanding our shared history as a framework for navigating contemporary challenges.

About The Publisher

Welcome to The Book On Publishing

At The Book On Publishing, we believe in rewriting the rules of learning. Whether you're chasing your next big idea, building a better life, or simply curious about what should have been taught in school, you've come to the right place.

We're a platform built for dreamers, doers, and lifelong learners, offering bold, practical books and tools that empower you to take charge of your journey. From real-world skills to mindset mastery, we publish the book on what matters.

No fluff. No lectures. Just what you need to know, delivered with clarity, purpose, and a spark of curiosity.

Start exploring. Start growing. Start writing your story.

Read more at https://thebookon.ca.

Acknowledgment of AI Assistance

Portions of this book were developed with the support of AI. While every word has been carefully reviewed and refined by the author, AI served as a valuable tool for brainstorming, editing, and structuring ideas. Its assistance helped accelerate the creative process and clarify complex topics.